## STRONGER MAN NATION
### Biblical Manhood Series

### LEADER WITH A CROWN TO WIN

Adam James

*ATHLETE: Leader With A Crown To Win*

Copyright © 2023

Published by Grace City Publishing

All rights reserved. No part of this publication may be reproduced in any form, stored in a retrieval system, or transmitted in any form by any means—electronic, mechanical, photocopy, recording, or otherwise—without the prior permission of the publisher, except as provided by United States of America copyright law.

Editorial Team: Luke Ellington, Chief Editor; Karis McPherson, Art Director; and the Proofreading Team.

Printed in the United States of America.

To the Stronger Men of Grace City Church—the men I run with.

To the sons and daughters entrusted to us,
who will carry the baton on the next lap.

To my wife, Erin, my best friend and the secret sauce in my life,
I love you!

You then, my SON, be strong in the grace that is in Christ Jesus. And the things you have heard me say in the presence of many witnesses entrust to reliable men who will also be qualified to teach others. Join with me in suffering, like a good SOLDIER of Christ Jesus. No one serving as a soldier gets entangled in civilian affairs, but rather tries to please his commanding officer. Similarly, anyone who competes as an ATHLETE does not receive the victor's crown except by competing according to the rules. The hardworking FARMER should be the first to receive a share of the crops. Reflect on what I am saying, for the Lord will give you insight into all this.

2 TIMOTHY 2:1-7

# STRONGER MAN NATION

Welcome to Stronger Man Nation. We are more than a band of brothers. We're a movement of men committed to making good battle with our lives.

---

# STRONGER MAN NATION
## Biblical Manhood Series

Weekly devotions and discussion tools designed to build and strengthen men.

Ideal for individual or group study.

**SOLDIER:** PROTECTOR WITH A BATTLE TO FIGHT

**FARMER:** PROVIDER WITH A FIELD TO WORK

**ATHLETE:** LEADER WITH A CROWN TO WIN

**SON:** LOVER WITH A FATHER TO PLEASE (Coming Fall 2023)

# CONTENTS

Acknowledgments..................................................................................................1

Introduction............................................................................................................3

How To Use This Book..........................................................................................7

**WEEK 1** STRONGER MEN LIVE LIKE ATHLETES (2 Timothy 2:5).........................8
    *From A Stronger Man: Don Odegard*

**WEEK 2** A STRONGER MAN LEADS AND FOLLOWS (1 Corinthians 11:1)..........20
    *From A Stronger Man: Chris Foreman*

**WEEK 3** KNOW THE RACE YOU'RE RUNNING (Acts 20:24)..............................32
    *From A Stronger Man: Larry Lehman*

**WEEK 4** RUN TO WIN! (1 Corinthians 9:24)......................................................44
    *From A Stronger Man: Dave Haehl*

**WEEK 5** TRAIN FOR MORE THAN A FADING CROWN (1 Corinthians 9:25).......56
    *From A Stronger Man: Jake Kragt*

**WEEK 6** DISCIPLINED OR DISQUALIFIED (1 Corinthians 9:26-27)....................68
    *From A Stronger Man: Brent Frank*

**WEEK 7** IT'S A TEAM SPORT (Romans 12:3-8)................................................82
    *From A Stronger Man: Aaron Binger*

**WEEK 8** THROW OFF EVERYTHING THAT HINDERS (Hebrews 12:1-3).............94
    *From A Stronger Man: Doug McGill*

**WEEK 9** PRESS ON TOWARD THE GOAL (Philippians 3:12-14).......................106
    *From A Stronger Man: Ka'ala Knell*

**WEEK 10** PREPARE YOUR MINDS FOR ACTION (1 Peter 1:13-15)....................118
    *From A Stronger Man: Jeremy Stumetz*

**WEEK 11** IT'S NOT HOW YOU START; IT'S HOW YOU FINISH (2 Timothy 4:7-8)....130
    *From A Stronger Man: Jeff Leavitt*

**WEEK 12** SETTLE THE GLORY ISSUE: ALL IN, ONE NAME (Revelation 4:9-11)....142
    *From A Stronger Man: Norris Williams*

Additional Questions For Discussion..................................................................156

Ways To Practice Being An Athlete / Leader......................................................158

# ACKNOWLEDGMENTS

Once again, it is the commitment and generosity of the people of Grace City Church, with the commissioning of our incredible team of elders, and the support of our gifted staff team, that has made this project possible. Pastor Josh's vision and desire to free me up to produce content for men and for our church family is a wonderful blessing. It's good to be Grace City! Thank you to those who intentionally prayed for me during this third sprint. Your texts were as timely and needed as your prayers. Thank you to the men who shared pieces of their testimony, experience, and insight for each chapter. So many great lessons from the fields of friendly strife and the experiences you've had! Thank you, again, specifically, to the tireless Karis McPherson and all her designing and formatting to craft a visually and aesthetically pleasing and accessible resource. To the myth, the man, and the legend, Luke Ellington, who quarterbacks timelines, editing, printing, and production—and whose genuine excitement for these tools is motivating and inspiring. To the group of men I meet with every Friday at 5:30a, thanks for digging in each week and working it out in real time. Thank you to the many coaches and teammates who gave me the experiences through sports that have shaped my life in such profound ways. I only wish I would have known then the things I write about today. When we were living those moments, they were an echo, pointing to so much more. Which leads me to give thanks, above all, to Jesus Christ, who ran the race with perseverance and who, for the joy set before Him, endured the cross and sat down at the right hand of God. Put me in, Coach! "All In, One Name."

# INTRODUCTION

## To every man reading this: *You have a race to run and a crown to win.*

You don't have to be physically gifted, naturally athletic, or participate in organized sports to be an athlete. God put you in a spiritual race and calls you to compete to the finish.

In this way, God made men to live with the mindset of an athlete and calls men to fulfill the role of a leader.

*"And from that day on, wherever I was going, I was running."*

Forrest Gump got that much right.

The Word of God is clear: Men were made to run (1 Corinthians 9:24-27).

To run the race of faith. Run to win. Maintain integrity. Make it to the finish. Keep the faith. Win the crown (2 Timothy 4:7-8).

Athletes are runners, winners, and leaders.

I was not a great athlete, but I grew up loving and playing sports. I played small town high school sports (like 8-man football small!). I played a lot of AAU basketball and a little community college basketball. Even then, I mostly cheered on my teammates. I played on some good teams and had some amazing experiences that marked my life. But every one of the stronger men who provided a testimony for this book accomplished far more than me in their athletic endeavors. I'm grateful for their contributions and I know you will be, too.

Even limited experience in athletics was enough to impact me deeply, in both good and bad ways.

Competition taps into the heart of men. Some suppress it. Some over-express it. But it's there. You want to win. At just about everything. Whether playing cards or wrestling with your kids; driving in traffic or walking through an airport; growing your business or arguing with your wife; handling the TV remote or playing a "fun" round of Pictionary with family during the holidays.

Admit it. You can participate in a meaningless game of just about anything and it doesn't take long to get fired up.

That "juice," that "drive," is a part of what it means to be a man. Yes, it's been twisted and corrupted and distorted by sin. Yes, it can be destructive and idolatrous and juvenile. Of course, there are totally pointless and stupid expressions of it and selfish motivations for it. There's a real dark side—as there is with all of God's good gifts. But the design and hardwiring is there on purpose, and we suffer if we don't understand and cultivate the redeemed intention for it.

We need to understand and reclaim the redemptive purpose of man's natural drive to compete and lead. When that energy is harnessed by the character of Jesus, it becomes a blessing to everyone and everything that man influences. "When men get stronger everything gets better."

We live in a day when strong men are accused of being toxic. In actuality, it's the dark side of weak and passive men—the abdicating of strength and leadership—that causes greater damage than overly aggressive and arrogant expressions of manhood (even though that's what gets most of the press). There's no excuse either way. Sin is destructive and harmful. I'm not excusing the overly competitive jerk. Or the heavy-handed brute. God will not be mocked, and He will deal with the arrogant and abusive. But the alternative is not to emasculate men and cut out one of the essential chambers of the heart of manhood. That's always the tactic the enemy takes. That's the war playing out in our culture today. *But don't throw the baby out with the bath water.*

We need men to be leaders who strive to win. Today, as much as ever.

The competitive drive in boys doesn't need to be reduced or removed— it needs to be redirected and redeemed. Boys need to become the kind of stronger men and leaders this world needs. Women, children, families, churches, businesses, communities, states, and nations need stronger men who know what it is to run hard and lead as men according to God's principles and Christ's character.

Throughout this Biblical Manhood Series, we are looking at four of the primary images God has given in His Word that make up what it means to be a man. Right from the pages of 2 Timothy chapter 2, as the Apostle Paul calls Timothy to be a stronger man. He calls him to live and lead like a Soldier, Farmer, Athlete, and Son.

## Men are made and called to be protectors, providers, leaders, and lovers.

# Warriors, workers, winners, and worshippers.

# Welcome to Stronger Man Nation.

We're all about becoming and building those kind of men. To bless women, children, the Church, and the world around us.

So get ready to lift some weight, do some reps, and break a sweat. Men don't grow and get stronger in any area of life without intentional training. Just like athletes. The virtues and attributes that go into the life of a committed athlete are the same qualities it takes to lean into your calling as a godly man.

We need discipline, hustle, drive, fight, grit, determination, perseverance, integrity, teamwork, preparation, follow through, execution, passion, focus, faithfulness, and more.

Men, like athletes, are those who show up at zero dark thirty or stay up to zero dark thirty and get after it when no one is watching. They train. They practice. They prepare. They give their all. They focus on the finish line, and they run through the tape.

Sports and athletics bring up all kinds of opportunities for character development and leadership lessons. Competition is filled with the language of glory and honor and praise, which tells you immediately, we are in religious territory that needs to be ruled by King Jesus in our hearts to get it right.

If you don't settle the glory issue in your mind and heart when it comes to the life and mindset of an athlete, you're a trainwreck waiting to happen and an absolute headache in the locker room. Everyone else knows it. It's time you figured out that you're not the MVP of the universe. That award has already been given. If you run to get all the applause, you're a weak boy on the verge of a great collapse.

There are great tensions to manage as we learn to run on the edge of a life fueled by a passion for God, running hard to the finish, learning to live "All In For One Name." That's when the freedom in the stride is sweetest, the exertion noblest, the aim highest, and the reward greatest.

This isn't about ego or manmade accolades. This isn't about chasing temporal dreams and joining the masses sacrificing to the $100 billion annual idolization of sports in the U.S. This isn't about re-living the glory days and propping up a hollow identity. No Uncle Rico's are needed. No million-dollar NIL deals are on the table.

Being a stronger man, like an athlete, is giving your all for the One who gave His all so that you could be rescued from Hell and the guilt and shame of living for selfish and trivial gain and glory. It's about joyfully laying down your life to lead others into a life of real victory that was secured by the true Victor and Champion, Jesus Christ, 2,000 years ago on a wooden cross.

Stronger men run to win a crown so they can lay it down at the feet of Jesus and bask in His glory for eternity, as part of the great crowd lifting up the true MVP.

So fellas, let's lace 'em up, stretch it out, grab a jersey, and line up. Quit looking at the cheerleaders and forget the old playbook. There's a new team with a new coach—a new race to run—and we're called to set the pace. Let's run to win the crown, together!

# HOW TO USE THIS BOOK

Scan the QR code below to watch a short tutorial on how to get the most out of your study.

## STRONGER MEN LIVE LIKE ATHLETES

Similarly, anyone who competes as an **ATHLETE** does not receive the victor's crown except by competing according to the rules.

2 TIMOTHY 2:5

There are three characteristics to the lives of athletes that Paul relates to the lives of Christian men and leaders.

#1 Running hard (aka competing).

#2 Running to win (aiming for the victor's crown).

#3 Following the rules, with genuine faith and integrity.

## FIRST, stronger men, like athletes, compete and leave it all on the field.

There's a certain kind of drive that is needed in the heart of every man if he's going to fulfill his calling to lead others well.

Just like a soldier is called to endure hardship, stay focused, and please his commanding officer (2 Timothy 2:4) and a farmer is called to work hard and pursue the harvest (2 Tim. 2:6), so too an athlete is called to compete with everything inside of him—striving to win the crown—and to do so according to the rules, so as not to be disqualified.

**"Similarly, anyone who *competes* as an athlete..."**

What does it mean to truly "compete"?

**Compete**: To engage in a contest. To strive. To strive to gain. To do your best. To contend.

**Contend**: To engage in a competition or campaign in order to win or achieve (something).

Paul knew that, in a very real sense, we are engaged in a great contest. He had seen the arenas in his day. The crowds roaring and cheering. The athletes striving and competing. The struggle. The fight. The stakes.

As he neared the end of his life, Paul looked to Timothy to continue on ahead, as if to say, "*Son, that's the game we're in. Keep the faith. Pass it on. Raise up more men. Keep going. Don't quit. Don't be disqualified. It'll take everything you've got. But stay the course.*"

Men are to be fully ***engaged*** in the race of faith. Engaged in the things of God with full force. Following Jesus is not a stroll in the park. It's not lollygagging toward whatever seems fun at the time. It's not a side hustle or part-time hobby.

It's a race. The gun has gone off. It's not time to be picking dandelions or counting clover leaves. Our little league days are over. It's time to be men.

*"Heads up, Johnny... RUN!"*

Can you see little Johnny look up, look around, recognize what's going on, and then finally decide to start running?

If we're honest, that's a lot of us men on a regular basis. *What am I doing again? Oh yeah, following Jesus, that's right. Oh yeah, I'm called to lead here, that's right.*

Let me ask you this. Currently, how focused are you in the race you're running? Would you say you're fully engaged? Eyes on the prize? Giving it your all?

Furthermore, what gets you truly fired up? What awakens the lion inside of you? That inner competitor. What brings out your best effort? Where in life are you truly exerting yourself to succeed?

Too many believe that to be a godly man or a Christian man is to check that competitive drive at the door. That somehow being a Christian man means we become (only) a docile, quiet, slow, gentle, soft version of a man. As if the grit and fire of a hungry competitor or ferocious contender is sinful and needs to be muted by the Spirit. The Bible begs to differ. Paul likens godly manhood and Christian leadership to the life of an athlete that "competes" and "contends."

If there's one thing our world needs more of today it's more men all-out competing and contending for godliness and righteousness and truth with more passion and more drive—not less. Individually and culturally. In every sphere.

## Let us strive to become those men and call more men to join us.

Yes, the fruit of the Spirit includes gentleness. Yes, the unhinged anger of a hyper-driven man is destructive. Yes, there's a kind of unhealthy competitiveness in the Body of Christ that has no place in our hearts or lives. But to be clear, the call of God on men is not anti-passion. It's not anti-effort. It's not anti-hustle or half-hearted running.

However many gears you've been given, Jesus gave them to you to drive them all. Pop the clutch, hit the gas, let's see what you can do. When there's only one lap to run, one life to live, there's only one way to run it. Full. On.

A stronger man channels and directs his internal drives, passions, and desires and aims them at a life of sanctified impact for the glory of God and the good of others. Make no mistake, when your feet hit the floor each morning, it's game on.

Brother, fan that fire into flame. Intensify that passion. And put it under the control of the Spirit of God so that it explodes off the block and refuses to let up.

Let me be clear, there's no right or wrong or better or worse personality or demeanor. Our diversity of gifts and strengths and temperaments is wonderful and God-given. But every man needs to cultivate a competitor's heart for the things of God in his own life and in his marriage, family, and church—contending for the gospel to advance in his generation.

The Christian life is not a sprint, nor is it a marathon. It's a relay. You and I are called to receive the baton and run our leg of the race, full-hearted, and then extend that baton to the next generation, until we all crash through the finish line into eternity.

## SECOND, stronger men, like athletes, run to win the victor's crown.

I'll talk more about this in chapter four, so I'll keep it brief here. Suffice it to say, the reward matters. No one enters the race to lose. We didn't enter the race to quit or be disqualified. All of those things are devastating possibilities. The good news is that, in Christ, the victory is secured. So long as we run to the finish. And the reward? Mind-boggling. Totally worth it! Keep in mind that the perceived value of a prize fuels the compelling effort of the participants. Paul even taps into the desire for reward and the fear of the loss of that reward when he says an athlete will "*not receive the victor's crown **unless** he competes according to the rules.*"

He's banking on the crown providing powerful motivation. And the threat of the loss of that reward is on the table as a tool to motivate obedience.

It's as if Paul is saying, "No child gets a piece of chocolate cake unless he finishes his chores." Suddenly, you find yourself motivated to finish your chores. Amazing how that works. Welcome to the human heart. And the Bible doesn't work around those motivations—it appeals to them and works through them, then transforms them.

He doesn't say, "Compete according to the rules—just because." Or, "Because I said so." No, he says, "No one receives the victor's crown unless they compete according to the rules." The rules are valuable because they are part of the means by which the victor's crown is secured.

The crown is at stake. I don't want to be disqualified. That's got my attention!

## THIRD, stronger men, like athletes, must compete according to the rules.

To win the crown you have to finish the race. For the race to count, you have to run according to the rules.

Here's the deal, brother. There's no shortcut, yet many will be offered to you.

Paul knows all about the dangers surrounding men and leaders. He's seen many fall. And he knows that without **GENUINE FAITH** and **PERSONAL INTEGRITY** you won't make it.

He's pulling no punches with Timothy or with you and me. Endure hardship as a soldier. Don't get entangled in civilian affairs. Run hard to the finish, compete according to the rules. Do not get disqualified.

There's a lot on the line. Your personal character and integrity will keep you in the race, but you wouldn't be the first and you won't be the last if you choose to blow it up and think you can get away with cheating.

I've sat across the table from men contemplating cashing in their integrity.

I've sat across from men who had already blown it with no interest in repenting or repairing the damage.

I've sat and listened to the sobs and waited for them to subside as a wife absorbs the shock and pain of marital unfaithfulness.

I've seen personal friends and former partners in ministry flush their character, lose their marriages, embrace false teaching, and cling to their addictions. I've watched men walk away from the faith.

I can tell you, firsthand, it's not worth it. The thrill subsides. The false promises fail to deliver. The heart hardens. They're out of the race.

## Brothers—whatever it takes—stay the course.

This isn't a call to perfection. And it isn't about try-harder, works-based salvation. Jesus Christ alone ran the perfect race. The race you and I couldn't run. We've all fallen short. In fact, that's part of what it means to compete according to the rules! You have to lay down your self-savior complex and any notion of self-made righteousness. Recognize that the only way to the Father is through Jesus Christ. It is only by grace alone through faith alone that any of us can come to God and receive the crown of life. And in this life, when we fall, we get up and run back to the cross. Running to the cross is the way we continue running the race of faith. There's a first time, but it's not a one-time bowing of the knee. We run the whole race of faith in the shadow of the cross, where Jesus died for our rule-breaking rebellion and self-righteous religiosity. At the cross, He gives us fresh legs to keep running.

Humility, repentance, and enduring faith. Those are the rules of the game.

The call of God on men and on leaders is to humble ourselves before God, repent of our sin, receive the gift of salvation available only through faith in Jesus Christ, and strive by His ongoing grace to live a new life of faithfulness empowered by the Holy Spirit.

This new life, in turn, is marked by increasing faithfulness, integrity, and purity as we persevere and make progress in the faith along with the people of God.

So, let's count the cost, brothers. Let's compete and contend to the finish with our faith and integrity intact. That's what it means to live like an athlete, a leader, a stronger man,

Let's stay the course!

"On the fields of friendly strife are sown the seeds that on other days, on other fields will bear the fruits of victory."

— Douglas MacArthur

ATHLETE

# FROM A STRONGER MAN

I have been married for 33 years, and I am a dad of two daughters (32 & 29) and one son (14). I was saved in 7th grade. However, I did not really have a broken heart for the Lord until the age of 42.

I grew up in a very abusive and dysfunctional home, which led me to have an intense desire to control my own destiny after high school...vowing never to return home. I was so desperate to be successful at something; I had an abnormal drive and took my work ethic and self-discipline to a very high level. For example, in high school during the season and off-season I would outwork EVERYONE during the week...more reps, more sprints, more time, better diet, and cleaner living. That wasn't enough. On the weekends, I would get the start times for all of the parties around town (Friday and Saturday nights). I would be sure to have cleats or spikes in hand and started my workout in the dark exactly when those parties were starting. I figured I MUST be getting better than the competition. Another example of my level of focus and discipline was illustrated in the 10 vows I wrote in high school..."never do this" and "always do that"...all of which were biblical vows. I was disciplined and focused.

That discipline paid off. I received a full-ride football scholarship to a Pac-10 (now Pac-12) school, received All-Academic Pac-10 honors during my time there and was later drafted into the NFL in the 6th round by the Cincinnati Bengals. Later, I was released and picked up by Pete Carroll with the NY Jets. I think I still have the fastest 40-yard dash time with the Jets (4.27).

After my football career ended, I took my discipline, hard work, and competitive nature to the business world. Through a number of blessings only God could be credited for; I ended up running a $200M+ agribusiness in the Columbia Basin. I knew the company was in trouble, but at the ripe age of 33 I hadn't developed the business acumen to know what a company looks like when it's facing bankruptcy. I had never felt so inadequate in my life, but I was committed. I gave it everything I had; 7-day workweeks, sleeping at the farm, and working on vacations. Even when I look back now, I cannot understand how our family survived other than by the sweet and tender heart of Jesus and a fiercely loving and supportive wife. At the end of a hard-fought 8-year run, we sold the business to Conagra Foods. In the final presentation, I recall the final 5 years averaged 45% year-over-year profit gains. That's unheard of in the business world outside of tech and startups.

The deal is never done until the money is in the bank. So, the day the banker called to tell me the money hit the account,

I went out and celebrated with my family...I wish. No, I hung up the phone and walked out of the kitchen, sat on the couch, and wept and wept. You see, my wife was in Hawaii on a trip with her sister, who went in my place. She was deciding whether or not to divorce me. My relationships with my daughters were more strained than they would be willing to admit. About two minutes after I sat down on the couch, the 10 vows came to mind—a physical bright light hit me, and I couldn't open my eyes. I had broken every vow but one. How could such a "good" kid end up like this?! It was 29 years in the making. I had mistaken God's patience for His approval.

What went wrong?! I had gone to church; I had done the Bible studies and I had given money to the church. I realized two things at this point in my life: 1) I realized that I could not walk in God's Spirit by self-discipline alone. I needed to be broken by my own sin and I needed to see my need for a Savior. Hard work and self-discipline, while important, aren't enough. I know I was saved by Jesus in the 7th grade, but I had a high pain tolerance, and I was unwilling to loosen the grip on my life. I wouldn't let Jesus have the wheel, so to speak. 2) I felt undeserved love for the first time in my life...from my wife. My heart was opened, and the Lord spoke into the deepest parts of my damaged heart. I could loosen the grip finally. It was ok...nobody was going to desert me. Here, the healing began. What a freeing feeling to be completely known, accepted, and loved.

**My self-discipline is still quite intact, but the fuel is no longer fear and anger —it is deep gratitude. Gratitude that God patiently spoke through my wife to show me His acceptance, and that He turned my eyes and heart to Him!** Today, God is my Father, the Holy Spirit is my Helper, and Jesus is my Savior. Full stop. My wife's love and trustworthiness broke my heart and Jesus filled it with Himself! I am still growing in Jesus, and I will until the day I die. Join me!

Compete like an athlete fueled and motivated by gratitude. If you don't have that gratitude, pray for it. I'm not sure how that prayer will be answered in your life, but it will be answered, and you can rest assured He will be glorified. You will find rest and those around you will be amazed at what they see. Stay in the game.

# Don, 56

ATHLETE

# REFLECT & DISCUSS

1. What is your biggest takeaway from this chapter? From the testimony?

2. What is your personal experience with sports and athletics? What was helpful and what was unhelpful about your experience?

3. How does considering the mindset of an athlete help you understand and think about stronger manhood?

4. Discuss the importance/role of effort in the Christian life. In what ways is effort good and in what ways can it be negative or misunderstood/applied?

5. Discuss the importance of genuine faith and personal integrity. What should we do when we sin and fall short? Can integrity be restored? What does that look like?

_____
_____
_____

6. What would you say are the greatest threats/temptations that you face when it comes to matters of integrity? How do you fight those?

_____
_____
_____

7. Where do you need to currently "pick up your game" and step up your leadership in your life?

_____
_____
_____

# TAKE ACTION

- If you're not in a Stronger Men group currently, identify and recruit 2-3 men you could read and discuss this material with weekly for 12 weeks. Be a leader, make it happen. If you are already in a group, think of 1-2 additional men you could invite to join you. Consider starting a second group, if needed, and leading them.

- Write out a current list of your roles (husband, father, son, brother, student, employer, employee...) and identify **ONE** next step you could take to improve your leadership **IN EACH ROLE**.

- Which role needs the most attention or increased effort currently?

## A STRONGER MAN LEADS AND FOLLOWS

# FOLLOW ME AS I FOLLOW CHRIST.
**1 CORINTHIANS 11:1**

# Leadership.

Very few words and topics have been so thoroughly studied and explored and written about across history. There is an endless library of books being written about leadership, great leaders, and the qualities that make up great leadership.

According to a 2019 Forbes article, US companies and individuals spend $166 billion annually on leadership development. Globally, it's a $366 billion dollar industry, according to the same article.

Leadership is a big deal.

John Maxwell, arguably one of the foremost experts on leadership in the 21st century, with over 75 best-selling books on leadership and 30 million copies sold, boils down the essence of leadership to the following definition: "Leadership is influence, nothing more, nothing less."

He also says, "Everything rises and falls on leadership."

Jocko Willink, Jim Collins, Peter Drucker, John Wooden, and thousands more would all agree and have all made their own mark on the leadership landscape. Along with many, many other leaders of all stripes and experiences and perspectives.

As a man, you're called to lead and apply godly influence to those in your life as you embrace the role of what it means to be a leader. There's a lot rising and falling on your leadership.

The Apostle Paul was a great leader. Next to Jesus, he is perhaps the most prolific leader in the New Testament, in terms of influence and output, arguably surpassing Peter, James, and John, and giving us the majority of the New Testament churches and letters.

He penned these simple words that have profound implication for men of God everywhere. It's one of the greatest leadership principles and statements ever made.

## "Follow me as I follow Christ."

That's true leadership. Let's break it down.

## 1. Great leaders ARE ALSO GREAT FOLLOWERS.

It's been rightly said, to be good in authority you have to be good under authority. The best leaders understand the weight and role of being a leader and the impact it has on those who look to them and follow them. The best leaders understand the view from both seats.

And for men called of God, we aren't lone ranger leaders. We're taking our cues and patterning our leadership after the greatest leader, Jesus Christ. What kind of a follower are you?

## 2. Great leaders TAKE RESPONSIBILITY.

Stronger men own it. No excuses. No passing the buck. Be ready to say, "That's on me." "Follow me as I follow Christ" means "I am taking responsibility for my faith, for my relationship with the Lord, for my character and my actions. And for my impact on others." Weak men refuse responsibility. Great men embrace it. When the Lord came knocking in the garden in Genesis, He wanted to talk to Adam first. Adam bore the primary responsibility for his own integrity, his wife and family, and the job God gave him. Are you embracing your responsibility as a man—as a leader?

## 3. Great leaders SET THE EXAMPLE.

Stronger men don't just know the way, and they don't just point the way. They show the way. They know that whenever they are pointing a finger at someone else, they have three fingers pointing back at themselves. What they call others to, they themselves live out. Stronger men root out hypocrisy in their lives and leadership. Weak men often say the right thing but fail to do the right thing. "Do as I say, not as I do" is not the motto of stronger men. "Follow me as I follow Christ" is more like it. Are you setting the right example?

## 4. Great leaders CALL OTHERS TO ACTION.

The strongest leaders are always men of action who call others to action. Talk is cheap, execution is everything. "Follow me" implies movement. Action. I'm going somewhere, and I'm calling you to come along. Let's go. Don't just be a talker, and don't just be a hearer—be a doer. As NFL running back Marshawn Lynch famously said, "I'm all about that action, boss." Now we're cooking. Where do you need to take action?

## 5. Great leaders USE THEIR GOD-GIVEN INFLUENCE TO URGE OTHERS TOWARD CHRISTLIKENESS.

It matters which direction you go. The kind of man you become. There is a right way. I call it "North." Set your compass bearings North and always fight to keep heading North. The action of men should not be aimless. It's not about getting busy for the sake of

busyness. It's about expending energy and taking action in the right direction. Christ is true North, and great leaders and stronger men rally people to go North. Are you heading in the right direction? Or have you drifted from the path toward what is good, right, and Christlike?

## 6 Great leaders LEAD FROM THE FRONT.

Leading from the front means you're involved in the action. You're connected. You're accessible and relational. You're making decisions from the perspective of someone who is in the game. This doesn't mean you never step back and get a broader perspective. There will be times you step back to "work on" your marriage, family, team, organization—not just "work in" it. But men, as leaders, need to be accessible, connected, and involved. Jesus took on flesh and walked among us. He knew the game, He ran the race. He didn't stand far off, removed from the action. Neither did Paul. Don't unplug and just lob decisions like grenades from a distance. Stay in the action, rally your team, and lead from the front.

## 7 Great leaders INITIATE GROWTH AND PROGRESS IN THE FAITH.

Stronger men initiate. This is true in general terms, and in particular in the spiritual health, growth, and progress of those you influence

WEEK TWO

and lead. For decades, research has shown that it is largely the wives and moms who take their kids to church. "Men don't go to church." Or people will say, "Men don't read." That's a bunch of garbage! If your church has mauve carpet and pastel plastic flowers, and everything is pretty and soft, and a man isn't expected to open a book...that might be part of the problem. For far too long churches have appealed only to the feminine. Additionally, culture has pushed men into a brutish or boyish box with "dad" being culturally depicted as the simple, stupid, unsophisticated moron. But there's no excuse. The truth is that great leaders and stronger men prioritize and cultivate spiritual growth and take the initiative to read, grow, and pursue the things of God. We take our families to church, initiate conversations with our wives and kids, ask questions, and encourage and challenge others in our sphere to take the next step in their own spiritual growth. Don't just "go along." Lead! What does initiating in the things of God look like currently for you?

## 8 Great leaders SET THE PACE.

As a young leader in my early twenties, I first heard the phrase, "The speed of the leader is the speed of the team." I didn't understand it at first. What does that mean? It didn't take long to realize and to experience the truth of what it means. We don't just set the example, we set the pace. If you're disorganized, your team will often be disorganized. If you've got momentum, your team will have momentum. If you're dragging, your team will start to drag. The people in your life are taking their cue from you. Leaders establish and embody the culture of their team. You set the tone and you set the pace. How will you practice? How will you work? How will you encourage others? How will you instruct? How will you sacrifice your own comfort for the good of those you lead? Great leaders do the little things that keep them moving forward at the right pace. And great leaders keep their finger on the pulse of their team. Great leaders know when to push and when to pull back. You know when to pick up the pace and when to rest. If you see a problem with the team, first look in the mirror.

## 9. Great leaders EXHIBIT HUMBLE CONFIDENCE BUILT ON SPIRITUAL INTEGRITY.

Humility. Confidence. Integrity. These are the traits of great leaders and stronger men. "Follow me as I follow Christ" carries the ethos of those qualities. Paul knew he was a sinner and boasted in the expansive grace that it took to save him. In fact, he knew he was "the worst." Paul was the worst sinner he knew. The same should be true of you and me. And he was also confident in his new identity in Christ and was living a new and transformed life of integrity and faithfulness. His spiritual authority and influence in the lives of the churches he planted and letters he wrote regularly appealed to the integrity of his life and actions. He had a strong voice because he lived a true life. "You know how hard I worked among you." "You saw my way of life." Paul never hid his sin or failure of the past and he was open and honest about the difference Jesus had made in his life. He didn't let his past define him, and he didn't claim to have arrived. Only the gospel of Jesus Christ can produce that kind of leader and man. What's the status of those qualities in your life?

## 10. Great leaders SUBMIT TO A HIGHER AUTHORITY THAN THEMSELVES AND ARE ACCOUNTABLE TO THE SAME STANDARD AS THOSE THEY LEAD.

Great leaders and stronger men are not rogue, independent, or unchecked. They are not above the law or beyond correction. Great leaders are those who are submitted to a higher authority and don't play by different rules than those they lead. "Rules for thee, but not for me" is the game of weak men, not strong men. Great leaders have high standards, rise to meet them, and accept the consequences when they don't. In fact, the Bible says leaders will be judged more strictly than others, not less. Are you submitted to God and to spiritual authority in your life?

## Stronger men strive to be great, godly leaders.
To be willing, ready, and able to step up and say, with integrity and confidence rooted in the Lord, "Follow me as I follow Christ."

This is the attitude and aim of stronger men.

Can you say those words with integrity to the people in your life? To your wife? To your children?

All pursuit of great leadership starts and ends with Jesus Christ.

Jesus Christ is the ultimate definition and example of greatness and leadership. He perfectly embodied all of the greatest attributes of leadership and is the standard by which all true greatness and leadership should be measured. He IS the King of kings, Lord of lords, and Leader of leaders.

# FROM A STRONGER MAN

It was the Summer of 1992. I was a freshman in high school and was trying out at De La Salle High School for the #1 football team in the state of California. De La Salle had a 151-game winning streak from 1992-2003. All this to say, if you played football in California, De La Salle was the school to play for. I was one of 110 kids who tried out for 53 spots that year. That hot summer morning, as "Hell Week" 2-a-days started, the coaches told us something that is still burned into my brain. They told us that they didn't want to make cuts, they wanted us to quit so they were going to run us until we quit. In that moment, I made a deal with myself, that no matter how tough it got, how tired I became, or how overwhelming the task was, I would not quit. I didn't quit. After 2 weeks of the hardest I have ever worked in my life—to this day—I ended up getting cut from the team.

Reflecting on that moment 30-plus years later, I ask myself what were the factors that led me to the desire to win and not be a quitter. Well, I had a great example of a "winner" in my life and someone to follow. The most influential person besides Jesus in my life has been my father. My father was a leader. He was leader in our home, in our church, at work as a SWAT Team Leader, and he was a leader as one of my coaches in numerous sports leading up to my freshman year. And later, he coached me in football as a Junior and Senior. I wanted to be like him, and I was willing to listen to what he had to say. I saw that he was willing to humble himself before the Lord in the ways he taught, fathered, and coached me. My father led by example but also was being led by others that he sought after to be a better husband, father, SWAT team member, elder in our church, and coach for sports. I know this because I remember my dad telling me numerous stories about the men in his life that he was following. My father was willing to follow as he led many others in his life, including me.

Now fast forward to the summer of my senior year, I switched to the public high school where I lived and had the goal of being named to the All-League Team. Our head coach for the football team called me out in front of the team at the end of one of our summer workouts and acknowledged my hard work and dedication, ultimately rewarding me with a Squad Leader spot. Squad Leader for our team meant at the start of each practice and each game I was at the front, leading the others on my squad in stretching but symbolically leading so others could follow. Now how did I get to that point, you might ask. Well, the leaders on our football team the year before had mentored me, led me with what it looked like to be successful with the example of hard work and dedication. I still remember those players taking me under their wing, giving me their undivided attention, and pouring their knowledge and experience into me. But once again, the person that had the greatest influence on my success was my father. My father led me by dedicating hours of time playing catch, motivating me in the weight room, on and off the field, and writing me motivational letters that he would put in my lunch before I left for school that challenged me not only on the field but in life, especially where I was falling short. My senior year culminated with me being named All League and leading the league in interceptions.

I look back now at that time and know that many life lessons I learned about leadership on the football field I learned from following others in the midst of leading others. I have learned after 20 years in law enforcement (leading as a Field Training Officer, SWAT Team Leader, Commander of our Drug Task Force and Chief overseeing half of our department), along with being a husband and a father that it is imperative to have men in my life that I am willing to follow and also men in my life that I am willing to lead. I have learned to seek out and find men who are willing to hold me accountable, ask tough questions, and invest in my life. Some of these men have been down life's road a little longer and have been willing to share their own mistakes in the hopes of me not making the same mistakes they did. This process and these men also help remind me of the importance of following and submitting to the Lord in all that I do in all aspects of my life. **I have learned that humbling myself before the Lord and before others and being willing to follow, especially in areas that I am weak or falling short, is imperative to how I ultimately lead others around me.**

One of the greatest generals of World War II, George S. Patton said, "Wars may be fought with weapons, but they are won by men. It is the spirit of men who follow and of the man who leads that gains the victory."

Who are you following? Who are you leading?

# Chris, 45

# REFLECT & DISCUSS

1. What is your biggest takeaway from this chapter? From the testimony?

_____
_____
_____

2. Which leader(s) in your life have had the greatest impact? How?

_____
_____
_____

3. Which of the 10 main points stand out the most to you and why? Where do you think you need to grow the most in your own leadership?

_____
_____
_____

4. Humility. Confidence. Integrity. How can you strengthen and cultivate these qualities in your own leadership?

_____
_____
_____

WEEK TWO

5. *"Leadership is influence, nothing more, nothing less."* Do you like this definition? Why or why not? How would you define leadership in your own words?

_____
_____
_____

6. *"Everything rises and falls on leadership."* What is helpful about this sentence? Do you agree? Why or why not?

_____
_____
_____

7. When you consider the life and leadership of Jesus Christ, what aspects of His leadership stand out the most to you?

_____
_____
_____

# TAKE ACTION

- Send a text, email, or call the leaders who have made the biggest impact on your life. Thank them again and be specific about what it was about their life and leadership that blessed and impacted you the most.

- **HUSBANDS** Ask your wife to read this chapter this week. Then ask her: "How would you describe my leadership? In what ways do you think I'm being a good leader? In what ways do you think I could grow as a leader in our marriage and in our home?" (Wives: Be kind and honest. Husbands: Listen without correcting or arguing.)

- **FATHERS/SONS** Ask your children or parents "How would you describe my leadership? In what ways do you think I'm being a good leader? In what ways do you think I could grow as a leader? (Be kind and honest. Listen without correcting or arguing.)

# WEEK 3

## KNOW THE RACE YOU'RE RUNNING

However, I consider my life worth nothing to me; my only aim is to **FINISH THE RACE** and complete the task the Lord Jesus has given me—the task of testifying to the good news of God's grace.

ACTS 20:24

Do you know the race you're running? The game you're playing?

When my oldest son was 6, I did the dad thing and coached his soccer team. That was an incredible experience.

I had never played soccer in my life, but hey, neither have 6-year-olds. I did a few searches on the internet for how to conduct basic beginner drills to use in practice and mapped out what I thought was a stellar plan and regimen for these little tykes.

The anticipation for the first game grew. My coaching debut. *Were the kids nervous? Ready?*

I may not have played or coached soccer before, but I'm a sports guy, a team sports guy, and a two-sport state champion in high school, I might add. Needless to say, I play (and coach) to win.

I'm quite sure my pregame speech was riveting and would have gone viral (had these kiddos owned cell phones and cared to post a video to their social accounts).

There I was, on a warm spring Saturday. Sun shining. Slight breeze. Green grass in a glorious park. Lawn chairs and blankets lining the sidelines with parents and grandparents and siblings waiting expectantly.

Cue the theme music. Start the slow-motion scenes of the grass, feet, and rolling soccer ball.

You know what happened? You probably do. A couple of the kids chased the ball, a couple skipped around in a circle together (Ben James, #2, pictured below), and one kid sat down and literally started picking grass. Eventually, I convinced my team to at least attempt to run in the direction of the ball.

It was as if they had no clue what game they were playing! Did I mention they were all 6 years old?

**Grown men can do essentially the same thing.** Imagine it from God's perspective!

*"Guys...the BALL is over THERE! The goal is that way! Do you know the game we're playing?? Quit eating the grass! Tommy, TOMMY... come here...remember what we talked about, Tommy. We're trying to put that soccer ball in that goal, let's go buddy, you can do it—go get it!"*

Oh the patience and perseverance of our Heavenly Father!

What's the goal? What's the point? What direction am I supposed to be running? We are so easily distracted.

Once again, the Apostle Paul provides a helpful example. He knew the race he was running. The task he had been given. And everything was being focused and leveraged to that end and for that purpose—the task of testifying to the good news of God's grace.

The Lord rang Paul's (who was called Saul at the time) bell on the road to Damascus (read Acts chapter 9) and his course was redirected and set. Jesus was done watching Saul going in the wrong direction.

He put a new jersey on Saul that said "Paul." He put Paul on His team. "You're on a new team now, Paul. My team. You're going to start running different plays. It's not going to be easy."

You may not have had a Damascus road experience, but the Lord has still been just as clear in His Word with the task He has given you. And though it may look different in our day, and from man to man given the distinctives of a man's gifts and vocation, the task is the same:

## "Testify to the good news (gospel) of God's grace."

Friends, if you're a follower of Jesus, you are running the race to testify of grace. You could call it the grace race. Your life exists to be a witness. To give testimony to the grace of God in your life. Someway, somehow, you have the job of telling others about Jesus.

Charles Spurgeon (19th century English preacher) said, "Every Christian is either a missionary or an imposter."

In Luke 8, Jesus sails across the sea to an island where he comes upon a demon-possessed man. This man has been tormented for years and is out of his mind. He's burned bridges, broken chains, gone mad, and run around the tombs naked. The demons know Jesus has stepped onto the scene and they start to freak out. Jesus, who had just calmed the wind and waves of a storm at sea, now demonstrates His power over the spiritual forces of evil as He proceeds to cast numerous demons out of this man. He sends the demons into a herd of nearby pigs, and they run off a cliff into the sea and drown. Now the people freak out and run off to tell the folks in town. As you can imagine, it caused quite a stir and reaction. When the people from town came out to see what had happened, lo and behold, they find the man from whom the demons had gone out clothed, in his right mind, and sitting at the feet of Jesus! A miraculous deliverance and redemption had taken place that changed this man's life forever. Sadly, the people were so freaked out by the display of Jesus' power and authority over evil, and by the collateral damage of the lost herd, they asked Him to leave.

But the man whom Jesus had healed had a different desire. He was finally free! He wanted to be with Jesus! He wanted to go with Jesus. He begged to go! But Jesus sent him away, saying, "Return home and tell how much God has done for you." So the man went away and told all over town how much Jesus had done for him. (Luke 8:26-39).

Your story of salvation may not seem as dramatic, but the spiritual reality of it is the same. We should feel just as much awe and gratitude and desire as the man set free. And we all receive the very same instructions from Jesus.

Apart from Jesus, we were all in a world of mess. Bound by our sin. Under the rule of the enemy. Darkened in our minds and separated from the life of God. We were dead in our sins, following the ways of this world and of the ruler of the kingdom of the air. Led by the spirit of disobedience. We gratified the cravings of the sinful nature, following its desires and thoughts. Like all of sinful mankind, we were by nature objects of wrath (see Ephesians 2:1-4).

The Apostle Paul wrote those words in Ephesians 2:1-4 to the church in Ephesus he had planted and the elders he was leaving in Acts 20.

## In **Ephesians 2:4-10**, Paul continues,

*"But because of his great love for us, God, who is rich in mercy, made us alive with Christ even when we were dead in transgressions—it is by grace you have been saved. And God raised us up with Christ and seated us with him in the heavenly realms in Christ Jesus, in order that in the coming ages he might show the incomparable riches of his grace, expressed in his kindness to us in Christ Jesus. For it is by grace you have been saved, through faith—and this not from yourselves, it is the gift of God—not by works, so that no one can boast. For we are God's workmanship, created in Christ Jesus to do good works, which God prepared in advance for us to do."*

WEEK THREE

We were, by nature, objects of wrath yet saved by God's grace! If you're a Christian, that IS your story.

## Our task is clear: TELL THE WORLD.

I remember the day I first read Luke 8:39 and knew that whether I went on to become an engineer or a sports broadcaster or a landscaper or a plumber or a teacher or a pastor...my task, my race, was forever marked by telling others what Jesus had done for me.

### I once was lost, but now I'm found.
### I once was blind, but now I see.
### I once was dead, but now I'm alive.
### I once was bound, but now I'm free.

*Jesus set me free. He changed my life. I'd love to tell you more about it. Got time for lunch sometime?* Believe me, no one is more surprised than me that I'm a pastor. The fact that I'm clothed (true story for another day), in my right mind, sitting at the feet of Jesus…??? It's wild! It's grace.

How many of you reading this, were you writing this chapter, could say the same thing? "I should not be here. I can't believe I'm still alive." I've heard it hundreds and hundreds of times. And I believe it. I know it in my own story. And it's too good to not share.

That's the game, gentlemen. That's the game we're playing. It's all about Him and all for Him.

Settle that issue in your mind and in your heart and look at everything and everyone through that lens. The clock is ticking. It's the 4th quarter. It's game time. Time to focus. No time to waste or spin around in circles.

Many men, even Christian men, wander through life aimlessly. They don't know the game they're playing; they don't know the race they're running; they don't know the task they've been given. They wander because they wonder, "What am I supposed to be doing?"

Or they are simply running a different race. Accumulating the wrong points on the wrong scoreboard that simply will not amount to a hill of beans in the end.

Many men cling to their life with a self-protective fear of the full implications of the call of God upon them. Are you afraid to surrender?

Without the confidence of knowing the aim of your life with deep rooted conviction, you will hold back and you will miss out.

Not Paul. "I consider my life worth nothing to me," he said. All his chips were in. Paul is a stirring example of a man on mission. A man on fire. A man with clarity and conviction and confidence and courage.

When you cultivate those qualities, in many ways, you become untouchable until the Lord is done with you. Undeterred. Unflinching. You're free to live fearlessly. You're free to live boldly.

I want to run with men like that. I've given my life to run with men like that.

Stronger men know the race they are running and the task they've been given. Let's run!

# FROM A STRONGER MAN

As an athlete, hard work and motivation has allowed me to achieve nearly all of the goals that I set for myself on the field. I attended high school in San Diego and remember, before my senior year, my head coach told me that I was not the caliber of athlete Division I (DI) schools were looking for and I should look elsewhere. Of course, I disagreed and with an aim of a DI school, I worked hard to prove him wrong. That day came when I donned the purple and gold jersey and ran out the tunnel at Husky stadium for the first time in 1991. This DI team, I proved I could be on, went 12-0 and won the national championship. As a red shirt freshman, I didn't play in a game that year; however, over the next two years I was able to move up the depth charts and realized that I could play with guys who would eventually make the NFL. Instead of driving me further, I felt as if I had completed the race that I had set out for myself. I had nothing else to prove and I reached my goal. My mind and desires had moved onto the next thing to pursue and achieve.

I realized that as an athlete I craved and desired the praise and accolades that came with success on the field. It was easy to work hard when motivated by the roar of the fans and the continual praising of your performance. This was instant gratification, giving me an identity based on my own strengths and abilities. Of course, in pursuit of the goals there were times when I did not perform well and instead of praising there were boos, yelling, and running. As a non-believer, my hard work and motivation only fed my own identity, which allowed me to move to the next race I decided to run.

I was raised in a Catholic home and was taught about God and heaven but never really saw the need. During high school, I rarely attended church and remember thinking that if the God and heaven thing were true, I could always put in some work into getting there. I met my wife in college and we both were living in and for the world. We were married a year after graduation and I watched as God opened her eyes and redeemed her. Although we were attending church regularly, I was not a believer and our first years of marriage were difficult. I had expectations that were selfish and unrealistic and foolishly thought that everything would come easy and marital and parenting success was guaranteed with hard work. The problem wasn't the lack of hard work rather there was a lack of proper motivation. In Acts 20:24, Paul worked hard proclaiming the gospel and was able to persevere because his motivation came from honoring God. **I was working hard to be a protector, provider, leader, and lover but my motivations were selfish, neglecting the spiritual side and our**

**marriage suffered. Without Jesus, I was not running the same race as my wife and was not willing to sacrifice my life.**

God was patient and long suffering as He slowly destroyed the self-proclaimed identity I was fighting to maintain, by opening my eyes to my pride, selfishness, and stubbornness. He showed me how I was pushing Him away by telling Him that I could handle things and I didn't need Him. God removed my disbelief and gave me a new identity as a chosen son and has continued His restoration work in me. It was not perfect on my side and I remember one night God freed me from the idea that there was value in my hard work and my abilities outside of Him. He revealed to me that I was still relying on my hard work to be able to take a blow (trials) and continue the race. He showed me that hard work without God as motivation was worthless. I finally understood God's grace as an immeasurable gift given to me that I can do nothing to work for and don't deserve. I am thankful for a loving wife and stronger men that God brought into my life as examples of men who work hard to protect, provide, love, and lead their families with a proper motivation of glorifying God. By the grace of God and His hard work, my wife and I have been married for 26 years and we have three God-loving children. I am daily working on this and am convicted to work hard on my relationship with God, my marriage, and my parenting to finish the race well and glorify God. I am thankful that in success and failure, I know that I have a Heavenly Father that loves me, accepts me, cheers me on, and provides me with the strength to finish the race well.

As an athlete, I know what it feels like to work hard and I continually pray that God will give me the strength and determination to work hard on the race God calls me to as a protector, provider, lover, and leader. Just as an athlete takes the field, I will take the field proclaiming God's truth and grace knowing that He has completed the work and invited me to participate.

# Larry, 50

# REFLECT & DISCUSS

1. What is your biggest takeaway from this chapter? From the testimony?

2. What is your favorite sport to play? Why? What is your favorite sport to watch? Why?

3. How and why did you choose your career path? Were there any other vocational paths you seriously considered? How did you narrow your choice and make your decision?

4. Clarity. Conviction. Confidence. Courage. What difference do these attributes make in a man's life? Describe a time in your life when one or more of these were present. Describe a time when one or more of these were NOT present.

5. How would you describe your life before you met Jesus? How would you describe your life now? Or how would you describe where you are right now in your spiritual journey?

6. What are the biggest distractions for you in your leadership at your home and workplace? What keeps you from being a focused man and leader? What are the biggest distractions for you personally when it comes to investing in your relationship with the Lord?

7. When you think of being a "witness" or "testifying" for Christ, what picture or image comes to your mind? What would that look like for you in your daily life? How strongly do you feel about that task?

# TAKE ACTION

Make a list of people in your life you believe the Lord wants you to be praying for. Spend a few minutes each day asking God to work in their lives. Track how many times you actually pray for them this month. What did you notice or experience during the month or at the end of the month? Look for opportunities to talk to those people and let them know you have been praying for them. How did those conversations go? How did those people respond?

# WEEK 4

## RUN TO WIN!

Do you not know that in a race all the runners run, but only one gets the prize? **RUN IN SUCH A WAY AS TO GET THE PRIZE.**

1 CORINTHIANS 9:24

ATHLETE

Remember the reality TV show "Survivor?" Apparently, it's still alive and running. How apropos. Contestants are taken to a remote location, put into teams or "tribes," and challenged to survive, not only the elements of physical survival (shelter, food, water, etc.) but also the tribal councils each week when one member of the tribe is voted "off the island." During the week, the teams compete in a series of tasks and contests to win various prizes and advantages that help them endure the elements and provide badly needed boosts of comfort or morale. Every episode, the host, Jeff Probst, explains the new competition and challenge, goes over the rules, and then, without fail, always asks the following tantalizing question: *"Wanna know what you're playing for?"*

He then proceeds to show them a lavish prize of some delicious food, comfortable accommodations, invaluable tools for survival, or a cherished opportunity to speak to a loved one back home. You can hear the collective reaction from both tribes. He has their full attention.

What's the point?

**When you know what you're playing for, and it's of true value, your heart is engaged, your motivation is activated, and your best effort is secured.**

**Effort and reward are linked.**

While it's true that personal effort, or doing your best, has an internal joy and reward of its own—which also makes the same point—there's no denying that the reality of an external prize, reward, or trophy at the end calls out the best in competitors. The anticipation of gain is one of the strongest psychological motivators. Even if it's just bragging rights.

## DO YOU KNOW WHAT YOU'RE PLAYING FOR?

How hungry are you for the prize the Lord is offering? Do you know what the prize even is?

More than any sentimental notion of heaven, carnal appeal to selfish glory, or generic reference to a "better place," you were made to know the mind-blowing joy of the unfiltered presence of God forever. He *is* eternal life!

The greatest "gift" of heaven is the Giver Himself—being in the very presence of God.

When you know that to be true, the thought of receiving the reward of His presence has the power to sustain you and propel you through any and every trial and hurdle you face. No sin, temptation, fleeting pleasure, or earthly reward is worth forfeiting the glory and greatness of the eternal reward of the all-satisfying presence of God.

**Those who know this priceless reward say things like:**

> *You have made known to me the path of life; you will fill me with joy in your presence, with eternal pleasures at your right hand.*
> **Psalm 16:11**

> *Taste and see that the Lord is good; blessed is the man who takes refuge in Him.*
> **Psalm 34:8**

> *Because your love is better than life, my lips will glorify you. I will praise you as long as I live, and in your name I will lift up my hands. My soul will be satisfied as with the richest of foods; with singing lips my mouth with praise you.* **Psalm 63:3-5**

> *Whom have I in heaven but you? And earth has nothing I desire besides you. My flesh and my heart may fail, but God is the strength of my heart and my portion forever.*
> **Psalm 73:25-26**

> *How lovely is your dwelling place, O Lord Almighty! My soul yearns, even faints, for the courts of the Lord; my heart and my flesh cry out for the living God.* **Psalm 84:1-2**

> *Better is one day in your courts than a thousand elsewhere; I would rather be a doorkeeper in the house of my God than dwell in the tents of the wicked.*
> **Psalm 84:10**

> *Praise the Lord, O my soul; all my inmost being, praise his holy name. Praise the Lord, O my soul, and forget not all his benefits—who forgives all your sins and heals all your diseases, who redeems your life from the pit and crowns you with love and compassion, who satisfies your desires with good things so that your youth is renewed like the eagle's.* **Psalm 103:1-5**

That's what we are running for! That will energize your running and pull out of your chest the greatest race of your life. To think about the prize is to fix your eyes on Jesus and run your heart out to the finish.

**Something this amazing is too good not to share!**

That's another prize in itself.

It is clear from the surrounding context of this verse that Paul's "prize" to "win" is also helping others meet, love, and follow Jesus.

He's running for his own prize, but he's also running for the prize of others being saved.

In the few verses above this week's focus text, **1 Corinthians 9:19-23**, Paul writes the following:

> *Though I am free and belong to no man, I make myself a slave to everyone, to win as many as possible. To the Jews I became like a Jew, to win the Jews. To those under the law I became like one under the law (though I myself am not under the law), so as to win those under the law. To those not having the law I became like one not having the law (though I am not free from God's law but am under Christ's law), so as to win those not having the law. To the weak I became weak, to win the weak. I have become all things to all men so that by all possible means I might save some. I do all this for the sake of the gospel, that I may share in its blessings.*

Paul is definitely concerned about and consumed with winning. Winning what? Winning souls! People! All types. Religious, non-religious. Churched, unchurched. Weak, poor, addicted, wealthy, respectable, influential—everyone!

**Following Jesus, running the race of faith, is not just about getting your own crown but helping others get theirs.**

A leader is someone who finds his success and joy in the success and joy of those he leads and those *they* lead. A leader aims to lift others up. As men, we are called to help, bless, and serve others in the process of helping them meet Jesus.

## Run to win the prize and run to win people, starting with your family.

Brothers, let it begin in your own household. Start with your own family! Have you won your family? Run to win! Win your sons! Win your daughters! Win your wife!

Yes, put your own oxygen mask on first. So that you can then help those around you—in your house, next door, across the street, at work. As many as possible.

Friends, the time is short. The need is great. The clock is ticking. The ball is in your hands. You're on the court. You're on the field. You're on the track, and the starting gun has been fired.

Paul is concerned and consumed with the eternal destiny and salvation of people. How often does it even cross our minds?

In the very next chapter and paragraph, Paul uses Israel as a warning to the Corinthians. They had a front-row seat and still missed it! So don't assume those who appear to know God, who give a little nod here or there, who attend church now and then…don't assume that those people are safe or saved. There are people who have a kind of generic knowledge about God and are around God but aren't actually saved. Just like Israel, who had all kinds of experience and proximity, yet most died in the desert and did not enter the promised land. Proximity is not the same as personal relationship.

The Bible says, "Make your own calling and election sure." Make sure. With yourself and with others. Don't assume. Double-check. It's the most important thing. It's the prize. Don't run for anything less.

What are you tempted to run for instead?

Too many men run for the wrong prize. What fake prize distracts you the most? How can you reset your course?

**What are the hurdles that stop men or slow men down from endeavoring to share their faith or win others to Christ? There are four big ones.**

Don't let these hurdles get in your way. Do whatever it takes to train yourself to jump over these every day. Make an honest assessment for which of these hurdles you run into the most.

## HURDLE #1: APATHY

"I'm not convinced or moved enough to take it seriously." "I'm consumed with other things." Check your heart. Get an eternal perspective. Refocus on reality. Apathy is short-sighted. And dangerous. You've lost sight of your own sin, the cross, Jesus, and salvation. You've drifted off course and the enemy has tripped you up. You're believing the lie that "it's not that big of a deal." Repentance brings renewal and refocus!

## HURDLE #2: LACK OF CONFIDENCE

"I don't know what to say." "I don't know how to bring it up." Far too many Christians, in general, and Christian men, in particular, don't have confidence in navigating gospel conversations. What do you say? How do you even go about it? Here's what is sad about that: brother, you are smart enough to figure it out. Who do you know that you could talk with to help you get equipped and grow in your confidence? Men can talk easily and quickly about things they love, things they enjoy, and things that are important to them. Men can talk about trucks and guns and gear and bait and business and markets and tools and sports with perfect strangers on a moment's notice. Or whatever your thing is. Yet we get tongue-tied and stuck when it comes to Jesus. Make Jesus your "thing" and you'll figure it out in no time. You don't need a PhD. In fact, initially, it's as simple as asking questions and listening.

## HURDLE #3: FEAR

"What will people think?" "What if they ask me a question I don't know the answer to?" "I don't want it to get awkward." If we let fear of rejection or awkwardness or failure or _____ keep us from talking to others about Jesus, we've lost sight of the prize. You've let the wrong fear take the lead. Push through the fear of man, with greater love that casts out fear. I'm not saying be obnoxious and robotic and pushy. Be the Spirit-filled version of you. Pray, look for opportunities, and lean toward boldness. You won't regret it.

## HURDLE #4: "THAT'S SOMEONE ELSE'S JOB."

"Someone else will do it." "That's the pastor's job." Actually, you're the plan. And if you're a follower of Jesus, it is your job. It's all our job, collectively. Jesus said, "You will be my witnesses." "Go and make disciples." "As the Father has sent me, I am sending you." This is actually good news! It's not a burden. It's a privilege—an incredible blessing. Have you ever led someone to the Lord? You're not alone if you haven't. Make it a goal! Ask the Lord to give you opportunities, open doors, and see what happens. Trust me. Give it time, pray about it, look for opportunities, take the first step, and see where it leads. On Team Jesus, everyone plays. Not only do you get forgiven and welcomed onto the team (which is mind-blowing), your number gets called and you get in the game! In fact, He has plays designed just for you. You don't just get on the team, you get the ball. And as you know, you miss 100% of the shots you don't take. Take the shot!

Run to win the prize, brothers. The presence of God! And run to win people. Let's take as many people with us as possible—starting with our families!

## When you know what you're playing for, and it's of true value, your heart is engaged, your motivation is activated, and your best effort is secured.

This is the mindset and lifestyle of stronger men who lead the way.

When I was asked to contribute to the chapter titled Run To Win!, I was assigned my scripture of 1 Corinthians 9:24 to reflect on. When I received this instruction, I shook my head with a smile as it could have only come from the Lord: That is, 42 years ago this month I gave my life to Christ and was baptized in the ministry of FCA, The Fellowship of Christian Athletes, whose theme verse is 1 Corinthians 9:24-27! It was with this scripture that my life was confronted by fellow believers and the Holy Spirit to examine what it means to really "Run to Win." The foundational principles I had been brought up in, now had eternal questions racing through my mind for me to wrestle with as it related to me, the person of Jesus, and my life here on earth.

Many of you have heard the saying, "It's not a sprint it's a marathon," describing something that will take lots of effort. Life involves both. We all have short sprints in our life that require intensity and drive, and an all-in push for short seasons at a time, but the focus here is the totality of our Christian life. It is more reflective of the time and effort involved in what it takes to win a marathon, doing it for the right end goal. A marathon is a ton of planning over long periods of time that also includes diligence, concentration, perseverance, and training—mentally and physically. The duration of the run pushes one's abilities to the edge. A marathon encompasses all tangents of our being and a constant drive that never quits.

Given Paul's analogy to the Corinthian church of athletic competition as it relates to our Christian life, we must ask ourselves some questions: Who or what are we training for? Who are we running for? Why are we competing? What is the prize I should be consumed with obtaining? What's the end game?

I once heard the analogy of the corporate worker who was "climbing the ladder" of the organization. Full on immersion for the company, complete buy in and dedication each and every day. Long days gone from home missing key components of family life and events. Hotels, trains, planes, and rental cars at a hectic pace for years on end all to make the cut for the next department and promotion. Yet years of sacrifice for the company come at the expense of others, culminating in the realization they have climbed the wrong ladder. This person has run to win but in the wrong direction, for the wrong reasons, and has not obtained a victorious life. Robert Burns, the poet from the 1700's, echoes the life gone sideways when he wrote, "The best laid schemes of mice and men often go astray and leave not but grief and pain." A pursuit of life outside of knowing the person and work of Jesus will result in this kind of despair.

**So how can we be sure we are running to win in the race set before us? We must have a proper perspective and purpose for all our endeavors.** Colossians 3:23 states, "*Whatever you do, work heartily, as for the Lord and not for men.*" The Westminster Shorter Catechism declares, "The chief end of man is to glorify God and enjoy Him forever." This is our ultimate goal. This is the orientation we must have to obtain the imperishable prize that God offers us. To love and serve the Lord with all our hearts and mind all the days He gives us breath is the only formula to assure that we are running to win.

# Dave, 61

ATHLETE

# REFLECT & DISCUSS

1. What is your biggest takeaway from this chapter? From the testimony?

2. What's the biggest / best prize you've ever won or been given? Tell the story.

3. When you think of Heaven, what comes to mind? Is it a motivating idea/thought or if you're honest are you somewhat uncertain or unclear? What about Heaven is appealing? What are some of the questions you have?

[Note: *If you're interested in exploring "Heaven" further from a biblical perspective, I recommend Randy Alcorn's book "Heaven." I also recommend the sermon series from Grace City Church titled "Life After Death."*]

4. Who first told you about Jesus? Who else has God used to encourage you in your relationship with God? How did they go about encouraging you or talking to you about those things? How did it come up?

5. Which of the four hurdles do you most relate to? How could you make progress in overcoming that hurdle this week? This month?

_____
_____
_____

6. How would you describe the current spiritual health and status of your family? What steps could you take to invest in and encourage your family spiritually

_____
_____
_____

7. Have you ever helped lead someone to the Lord? Tell the story

_____
_____
_____

# TAKE ACTION

Lead your family in Bible reading and out loud prayer this week. If this is already your practice, how can you grow, tweak, add, improve, or make it special this week or this month? If this isn't your practice, start this week. It's okay to start small—just start. Read the verses from one of the chapters of this book and share how it encouraged you. Ask for their feedback and thoughts. Don't be discouraged or deterred if there's not much discussion at first. Close your conversation with a short out loud prayer. It can be as simple as, *"Lord, thank you for my family, please bless them this week and help us all to get to know You better. Help me be the Leader You're calling me to be for my family. In Jesus' name, amen."* Report back to your men's group how it went. How often would you like to do this with your family? Make a plan. Lead the way!

# WEEK 5

## TRAIN FOR MORE THAN A FADING CROWN

Everyone who competes in the games goes into strict training. They do it to get a crown that will not last, but we do it to get

# A CROWN THAT WILL LAST FOREVER.

1 CORINTHIANS 9:25

Goals. Priorities. Motivation. Training.

**A fading crown vs. an eternal crown.**

Paul is asking an important question. If "strict training" is what men are willing to do and give and commit for a mere game, are we at least just as committed and devoted to the pursuit of righteousness and growing our relationship with God for His kingdom?

In this verse, Paul is arguing from lesser to greater. If athletes, who are only competing for a fading crown that will not last, will devote themselves day and night to strict training programs, how much more should we, as followers of Jesus, as godly men, be willing to train and prepare and practice spiritually, when the reward is so much greater—an ETERNAL crown!!

Training, effort, commitment, focus, pursuit, excellence. How much more should these words and realities mark our pursuit of the things of God as they do our pursuit of the things of this world?

And yet, too often, tragically, that is not the case.

Let's be honest, nowhere is this as prevalent and visible as it is in the world of youth sports.

Sports, like all forms of worldly pursuits and successes, can be a great gift but makes for a terrible god. The idolatry of the fading crown of sports needs someone to call balls and strikes. Let's be stronger men who are leading our homes and keeping worldly pursuits in their place.

## Leverage sports and steward it for life lessons, leadership reps, community, mission, and spiritual growth? Absolutely. But don't let the tail wag the dog.

Holding the line, by keeping earthly and eternal values in their place, requires disciplined and focused leadership from stronger men.

The far-too-common reality is the elevation of the lesser and the sacrifice of the greater. I watch it play out in people's lives all the time and I know it in my own story.

**Here's a little more of my own journey with sports.**

I grew up playing A LOT of basketball. From 2nd grade all the way through my freshman year of college, it was essentially year-round. School ball plus AAU tournaments around the region and state, and even three national AAU tournaments. From Yakima, WA to

WEEK FIVE

Oklahoma City, OK, to Winston-Salem, NC (Wake Forest University), and a Basketball Congress International (BCI) tournament at Arizona State University in Phoenix, AZ.

I played in some of the same tournaments as future NBA players like Jermaine O'Neal, Mike Bibby, Desmond Mason, and I even played in a game against Luke Walton (and he only scored 16 points on us). I met and got my picture taken with Rick Pitino at the AAU National Tournament in North Carolina when he was coaching at Kentucky.

When I was in middle school, in 6th grade, we played something like 85 basketball games that year. That's more than an entire NBA season. And that doesn't count practices. It's really pretty remarkable when you start to add it all up. Hours and hours in the gym and on the road. Gas, food, hotels. Tournament fees. Jerseys. Shorts. Shoes.

I have some amazing memories. Sports gave me some incredible life experiences and greatly shaped my life. A lot of people put in a lot of time, work, and money.

As far as our athletic goals were concerned, it paid off. We did it. We qualified for nationals. But really, all of the AAU ball was just training and preparation to pursue the state tournament and state championship in high school basketball. Which we achieved my senior year. In fact, we won the state B championship title in both football and basketball.

In my junior year, we were the first boys team in the history of my high school to qualify for the state basketball tournament. The first team ever. There was a great sense of town pride and accomplishment. As my coach would say, *"For every Billygoat (yes, our mascot was a Billygoat and I'm proud of it!) who ever laced up a pair of high tops, this is for them too!"*

We ended up finishing 7th place my junior year. I finished the tournament tied for the most 3-pointers made in the state tournament that year. It was special. Our team also set a record that year for the most points in a single game in B tournament history, 96, and I believe that record still stands today.

Then came our senior year. The anticipation was high. We were ranked #1 all season long. We hit one speed bump in districts and lost to a team that we ended up playing again a few days later and beat by 40. So, we headed back to the state tournament. It was the first year in the new Spokane Arena. We were heading to Spokane with one loss and a lot of expectations. Without belaboring the story further, four games later, we were cutting down the nets and lifting the gold ball as the 1996 state champions. We put up 30 points in the 4th quarter to blow the game open and pull away with the title, 77-51. We finished the season 29-1. This was just on the heels of winning the State B-8 Football Championship, 76-20, a few months earlier and completing a 12-0 season. We were just the 4th "B" school at that time to win the state tournament in both football and basketball in the same year.

All that practice, all those games, all those road trips, and tournaments finally paid off. 11 straight years. From 7 years old to 18. 2nd to 12th grade. We did it. State Champs. And as my coach said at the time, "No one will ever be able to take that away from you. For the rest of your life, you'll always be a state champion." And it's true. There's something fun and special about winning. It feels good to win! And to have a hand in helping your team win? Exhilarating!

But here's my regret: I didn't know Jesus. I wasn't walking with the Lord. All that sacrifice, all that commitment, all that time, energy, and money. All that "success." And yet, those were also sadly, the darkest times of my life. I was chasing the wrong crown. If it's possible to have both fun memories and regrets, with a tinge of sadness, that's what I feel.

I went on to play basketball in community college, and it was in that freshman year at college that Jesus grabbed ahold of my life. And when He did, for me, sports had to go away for a while. Sports had definitely been an idol in my life.

As I began to experience my new life in Jesus and the thrill of being set free from my sin — I was excited to tell others about what Jesus had done in my life and I was given an opportunity to speak at a youth rally at my hometown church. I remember part of that first "sermon" I ever preached. I was 20 years old and still less than two years removed from winning back-to-back state championships in my senior year. As I told those students about what Jesus had done in my life, I said, "**Winning a state championship is great, it was a ton of fun, but it doesn't even come close to comparing with the reality of HAVING YOUR SINS FORGIVEN!!**" I literally jumped off the short stage and thrust my hands in the air landing in the center aisle of the first few rows of this countryside church filled with 100 students. I think I woke some of them up!

I still feel that way! Nothing compares!

The joy of knowing Christ far surpasses any athletic or worldly achievement. Small town or big city. 8-man or NFL. One crown fades. One Crown lasts.

Paul isn't saying you can't or shouldn't pursue worldly success. But he is saying you definitely shouldn't ONLY seek worldly success nor should you seek it at the expense of eternal and spiritual health. He told Timothy in **1 Timothy 4:7-8**:

> *Have nothing to do with godless myths and old wives' tales; rather, train yourself to be godly. For physical training is of some value, but godliness has value for all things, holding promise for both the present life and the life to come.*

**My honest question is this:**

## If we'll invest hours, years, sweat, tears, and thousands of dollars to pursue the goal of lifting a gold ball, or having a sculpted body, what will we do for the goal of godliness?

What will we give for more people to meet Jesus, more churches to get planted, and more men to get stronger? What will we do to grow in the faith and lead others to the Lord?

Will we train just as hard to know and handle the Word of God? Will we work just as hard to spiritually equip our sons and daughters to carry the torch of the gospel in their generation?

These are honest questions. And I know they're not mutually exclusive. Sports aren't "bad," they can totally be a means of investing in the kingdom of God. And physical training and health is indeed valuable and shouldn't be neglected. Yes and amen.

The fact remains, and Paul nailed it—this world goes hard after temporary crowns. He throws the gauntlet down. He says, that's what "they" do. But "we" go into strict training to get an eternal crown. Well, do we? What does that look like in your life?

Are you bringing a championship athlete's level of commitment, effort, and mindset to your leadership and investment in eternal things?

If you're pursuing sports as a young man reading this, or a dad or grandpa who is coaching and investing—is your eye on the eternal crown as you go about it? Are you leveraging your platform and relationships to instill kingdom values and rewards?

One of the great tactics of the enemy is to get you to intensely pursue anything and everything as long as you downplay, minimize, ignore, or put the things of God on the back burner.

What is the enemy tempting you to pursue or idolize? Is there anything that needs to be put back into perspective and focused and leveraged for the Lord instead of competing with Him in your life?

Don't substitute earthly things for eternal things. Don't elevate earthly things over eternal things.

It won't be worth it. It won't matter in the end. Well, it will matter in the end.

Does it matter if you "win" in the world but lose at home? Or lose your soul?

## Brothers, if you win in worldly pursuits but don't walk with Jesus, you lose.

Jesus asks in **Mark 8:36**, "*What does it profit a man to gain the world but lose his soul?*"

Goals. Priorities. Motivation. Training.

Take an honest look at the sacrifices and commitments you are making and the goals you are pursuing. Are your priorities in line with an eternal perspective?

Are you training for the crown that lasts?

That's what stronger men do. With all their might.

> "It's not the will to win that matters—everyone has that. It's the will to prepare to win that matters."
>
> — Paul "Bear" Bryant

ATHLETE

# FROM A STRONGER MAN

Growing up, sports were my identity. They were what I lived for and how I got my value from others. Growing up in a small "B" school town, most everything revolved around what the high school sports teams were doing. I always dreamed of playing college football. The last guy to get a Division I football scholarship from my town was 20 years before my senior year in high school. I had a goal, worked my butt off, and did it. I earned a scholarship to Eastern Washington University and played for 5 years. I never was the strongest or biggest or most talented, but I earned playing time and earned All-Conference honors my senior year.

Sounds like a great story with a happy ending, except my identity was found in my athletic achievements instead of God. I wasn't a believer. I knew of God, but not the God who saves. I grew up going to a religious Lutheran church that didn't do much to cultivate my faith and, if anything, made me resentful. My girlfriend, now wife (thank God!) invited me to a college night at a church in Spokane. I didn't want to go, but God had a different plan.

I walked in and the college pastor who happened to play minor league baseball came right up to me and said something that altered the course of my life. He said, "Jake, it's so good to meet you! I'm glad you're here and I know what it feels like to be in a locker room where you are the only one who loves Jesus!" Talk about a Holy Spirit punch in the gut. I felt frozen and never more convicted. I wasn't at all who he thought I was. I was a fraud. I gave my life to Christ that night and have never looked back.

**I spent years of my life struggling with feeling alone, depressed, and not good enough. When my value came from athletics, it went up and down based on my performance. When I became a believer, it didn't matter whether I had 5 sacks or rode the bench. His blood covered me. His grace was sufficient. I went from dead to alive.** My new community of brothers and sisters in Christ was better than anything I could have thought or imagined.

My focus now is continuing to seek to grow in my relationship with Christ and I am regularly challenged to be a humble leader and a godly man as I love my wife and raise our two young sons and daughter. My prayer for my kids is that they can rest in knowing Jesus is in complete control. I am teaching them to work hard, be disciplined, set goals, be good teammates, and through athletics, I pray the Lord will be glorified.

As a chiropractor and business owner I'm passionate about leveraging my career and business to bless others and further His Kingdom. My desire is for others to know and experience the abundant life that Jesus offers. After Jesus poured out His grace so freely over me, how could I not?! My life is His. What an incredible freedom there is being chained to Jesus.

# Jake, 36

ATHLETE

# REFLECT & DISCUSS

1. What is your biggest takeaway from this chapter? From the testimony?

2. What role did sports play in your life growing up? What was the "payoff" it gave you?

3. Were there other hobbies or pursuits that were (or ever came close to being) an idol in your life? What did it cost you (negatively speaking), what did you end up neglecting?

4. Describe a time when you set a goal that required ongoing motivation and training? What was that like? What did you like / not like about it? Is there anything like that in your life currently? Something you're training towards? Or something you'd like to train for in the future?

5. How do you practically work to prioritize your family and your relationship with God?

6. Do you have any regrets in life? Share an honest example. How should we handle our regrets in life moving forward?

7. How would you describe the benefits and dangers of youth sports? As a dad, how will you talk about these things and navigate these things with your kids? As a student athlete, how can you prioritize eternal pursuits in the midst of your athletic pursuits?

# TAKE ACTION

- Write yourself a new spiritual training plan this week. What should it include? How often? When will you start? What's the goal? Who will help you succeed? Lead the way!

- **FATHERS** Have any necessary conversations with your kids this week about the difference between the earthly and eternal crowns.

# WEEK 6

## DISCIPLINED OR DISQUALIFIED

Therefore I do not run like someone running aimlessly; I do not fight like a boxer beating the air. Rather, **I discipline my body** and make it my slave so that after I have preached to others, **I myself will not be disqualified** for the prize.

1 CORINTHIANS 9:26-27

Paul packed a lot into that little paragraph in 1 Corinthians 9:24-27. This is my third and final chapter unpacking the insights he conveyed in those four verses. Run to win the prize (1 Corinthians 24, chapter 4). Train for more than a fading crown (v. 25, chapter 5). And now, Paul emphasizes the need for self-discipline.

## Like an effective athlete, stronger men exercise self-discipline so that they won't be disqualified.

I'm not a naturally disciplined guy. I've heard some say that no one is, but I'm not so sure. I've known and observed a lot of men and leaders over the years, and it seems universally true that there are some categorical differences in dispositions among men. There's a reason all those personality tests exist. DiSC, Myers-Briggs, Enneagram, Strengthfinders, CVI, Crystalizer, and others.

Some men are visionary. Some men are systems-oriented. Some are big picture. Some love logistics. Some are early birds. Some are night owls. Some are wired more naturally toward steady routine and live their lives in a more organized and structured way. Others are more inspirationally based creative types that approach organization and structure a bit looser. Which direction do you lean?

There is no one size fits all "right" personality. All types of men can be highly effective and impactful leaders. All kinds of wiring come with their own built-in advantages and dangers. But no leader and no man is ultimately effective without self-discipline.

So, what is needed to become a disciplined man?

**Here are 6 KEY PERSPECTIVES that are critical to a disciplined life.**

## KEY PERSPECTIVE #1
## Discipline Needs Purpose

Donald Whitney, author of the book, Spiritual Disciplines for the Christian Life, said helpfully, "***Discipline without direction is drudgery.***"

There has to be a clear target, a clear sense of purpose for discipline in order for it to be maintained. For the Christian man, positively, that purpose is godliness (see 1 Timothy 4:7-8). The continual transformation of our character more and more into the person God intends us to be, which is to say, more and more into the glorious freedom of the image and character of Christ. Negatively, the purpose of discipline, as Paul warns himself and us in today's verses, is to avoid being disqualified. That's the brass tacks. There's a lot on the line.

Through discipline we direct and/or restrain our mind and energy into and away from specific actions for the purpose of godliness. Like a stagecoach driver with a team of hard-charging stallions, a disciplined man is the man who is hanging onto the reins and keeping the wagon on the road. He wants to get where he's going…alive!

The more we practice and maintain various disciplines of thought and action, the more consistent and predictable our response in various situations becomes. That's a mark of godliness and maturity.

Godly habits and self-discipline are a cornerstone and safeguard of stronger men and great leaders who are pursuing lives of generational impact. If that's your aim, keep reading.

## KEY PERSPECTIVE #2
## The Foolishness of Running Aimlessly and the Exhaustion of Beating the Air

Paul draws on the athletic example of a runner foolishly running aimlessly and a flailing boxer expending precious energy wildly beating the air.

The first is a picture of a guy running in circles. Or running with arms and legs flailing like a madman. Or that stagecoach running loose, unattended. Not a pretty picture or smooth operator. If we're honest, we've all been that guy. Aimless. Foolish. Without focus and direction. And when it comes to a real race, if you're not disciplined to stay in your lane, you'll quickly be disqualified. So it is in the race of faith.

Additionally, successful runners focus on eliminating any and all wasted motion. There's a fluidity and focus that help you glide down the track, over the hurdles, and maintain a steady stride. The more you can master that consistent gait and motion, the better the outcome will be. Aimlessness is foolishness. It's planning to fail. Instead, commit to a focused life.

In boxing, if you are not calculated and disciplined with your punches and defense, you'll end up gassed and quickly be defeated. A disciplined boxer can knock out a guy throwing wild, uncontrolled haymakers with one precisely delivered blow. I'm always amazed at the difference trained skill and discipline make in determining the outcome of a race or fight—it's so much more than raw talent, strength, speed, or ability!

I know many guys who are regularly exhausted (like I've been at times), and it often comes down to a lack of discipline. You think discipline is hard? Try flailing your way through life. Trust me, you'll really know exhaustion. You might be tired because you're just beating the air! What you need is clear direction and focus to give you a sense of progress and impact, which is energizing instead of exhausting!

In both scenarios—running and boxing—the undisciplined approach leads to burnout, disaster, and disqualification. The disciplined approach leads to energy, impact, progress, and victory. Or at least finishing the race/fight!

Both scenarios illustrate the power and need for focused, controlled action, which are critical aspects of self-discipline.

## KEY PERSPECTIVE #3
### The Power to Say "No" to Yourself and the Role of the Body

A man without discipline is a sitting duck. He's an easy target for the enemy. A man without discipline simply can't say "no" to himself. When the alarm goes off, he doesn't get up. When the cookies get opened, he can't stop. But a disciplined man has the ability to let his "yes" be yes and his "no" be no. He's free to say "no."

Our sinful flesh is never satisfied. Like fire, it is always ready to consume another piece of forbidden fuel. Sin is ready to grow and consume more. Our sinful flesh doesn't say "no" to temptation. Just as the land doesn't refuse to drink up the rain. Nor does the grave refuse to welcome another corpse. These never say, "Enough!" They always want more.

A man of Spirit-empowered discipline can exercise control over his desires and urges and has the power to say "no" to things his body craves. Whether it's sleep, food, drink, sex, power, anger, or all other varieties of the flesh-based desire. Lusts of the flesh seem to be such powerful voices and forces that daily devour countless men. Wide is the path that leads to destruction, and many go this way.

Men, it's important that we learn to exercise discipline in all areas of life. And notice, Paul is specific about bodily discipline because our sinful flesh includes urges and desires that are rooted in and connected to what we do with our physical bodies. There IS a connection between body and soul. Don't neglect either. One may come more naturally to you, but both are needed to be a godly, stronger man.

So, how are you doing with saying "no" to yourself?

# KEY PERSPECTIVE #4
## A Game of Desires: Strong or Weak? Old or New? A Liberating Truth!

C.S. Lewis captured it perfectly in his essay, The Weight of Glory, when he said:

> "It would seem that Our Lord finds our desires not too strong, but too weak. We are half-hearted creatures, fooling about with drink and sex and ambition when infinite joy is offered us, like an ignorant child who wants to go on making mud pies in a slum because he cannot imagine what is meant by the offer of a holiday at the sea. We are far too easily pleased."

That's a life-changing quote. Our desires are not too strong—they are too weak! We too often chase the cheap counterfeit pleasure of sin for immediate gratification instead of holding out for the greater pleasure of true joy in the path of faithfulness to Christ.

Sin is foolishness. It accepts the offer of filthy pond water by the dumpster instead of happily pressing on and waiting for the white sand and turquoise water of the beachside resort.

Discipline is never ultimately sustained by gritting your teeth and thinking you are refusing riches while holding out for poverty. It's exactly the opposite. Discipline is sustained by realizing you are unwilling to sacrifice the true riches of the blessing of God on your life by choosing the bankrupting curse of the enemy.

When that perspective clicks in, saying "no" comes much more freely.

Discipline is not refusing yourself satisfaction; rather, it's saving your appetite for that which is truly and gloriously satisfying.

In his essay, The Expulsive Power of a New Affection, Thomas Chalmers drops this gospel bomb that every stronger man must grasp:

> "There are two ways in which a practical moralist may attempt to displace from the human heart its love for the world — either by a demonstration of the world's vanity, so that the heart shall be prevailed upon simply to withdraw its regards from an object that is not worthy of it; or, by setting forth another object, even God, as more worthy of its attachment, so that the heart shall be prevailed upon not to resign an old affection, which shall have nothing to succeed it, but to exchange an old

*affection for a new one... From the constitution of our nature, the former method is altogether incompetent and ineffectual, and the latter method will alone suffice for the rescue and recovery of the heart from the wrong affection that domineers over it."*

How do you defeat an old sinful desire? Not merely by endlessly repressing and resisting it. But rather, by replacing and displacing it with a new holy desire.

The miracle of salvation does just that: God changes your "wanter." He gives us a new heart! The things you used to desire...you don't desire them any longer. Something greater has replaced those old desires! You now have new desires, new appetites.

The Christian life at its fullest isn't white-knuckling it to the finish line by raw self-denial. It isn't the exhausting work of starving—it's the gift of feasting at a better table!

God isn't a cosmic killjoy. He's a soul-satisfying Chef! He prepares a table before you in the presence of your enemies (Psalm 23:5)!

"Discipline" in light of this truth becomes an invitation to eat what is GOOD.

## KEY PERSPECTIVE #5
## The Freedom of Discipline

*"Discipline is the price of freedom and freedom is the reward of discipline."* – Donald Whitney, "Spiritual Disciplines for the Christian Life."

Just as a musician is only free to improvise on the piano or guitar after he has put in the hours of doing repetitive scales, so too an athlete is only free to display such competitive greatness and freedom after having put in tens of hundreds and even thousands of hours of practice and discipline.

Steph Curry displays the prolific shot-making freedom he does on the court because of the lifetime of discipline he's exercised in the gym when no one was watching.

Discipline is the price of freedom and freedom is the reward of discipline.

So, too, in the journey of godly manhood:

- The ability to freely quote or call to mind passages of sin-killing Scripture in the moment of need comes with the discipline of reading God's Word.

- The freedom of a joy-filled marriage comes with the discipline of faithfully loving, serving, and listening to your wife.

- The freedom to lead the family in soul-stirring prayer comes from the discipline of regularly praying alone, out loud.

Discipline in private paves the way for freedom in public. The Father sees what is done in secret and will reward us openly (Matthew 6:5-6).

## KEY PERSPECTIVE #6
## Talk is Easy; Action is Everything

Paul is well aware that he can talk the talk, and he knows that won't be enough. He's preached to others, but he's not out of the woods because of the things he knows or the things he's taught others. He, too, has to walk the walk. He can't afford to believe the press about "the amazing Apostle Paul." He can't make it without preaching to himself and living his own sermons. And neither can you or I. The victory is found in actual obedience.

Phil Rogers, the man who led me to Jesus when I was 19, would often say, "It's not how high you jump in your excitement for God, but how straight you walk when you come down." For a guy who talks for a living and can get plenty excited—but at times has struggled to follow through—those words landed and still ring in my ears.

In the language of sports, it's "put up or shut up." Or "If you're going to talk, make sure your game backs it up."

## Discipline is about action.
## So are stronger men.

Stay the course, brother!

*No discipline seems pleasant at the time, but painful. Later on, however, it produces a harvest of righteousness and peace for those who have been trained by it.* **Hebrews 12:11**

*For the Spirit God gave us does not make us timid, but gives us power, love and self-discipline.* **2 Timothy 1:7**

# FROM A STRONGER MAN

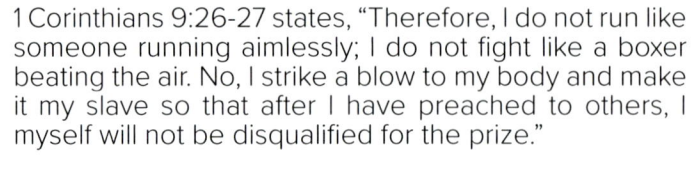

1 Corinthians 9:26-27 states, "Therefore, I do not run like someone running aimlessly; I do not fight like a boxer beating the air. No, I strike a blow to my body and make it my slave so that after I have preached to others, I myself will not be disqualified for the prize."

In this passage we see the apostle Paul referencing competition and the athletic arena to illustrate the importance of discipline and dedication in pursuit of living a Christian life. He underscores the importance of making fitness an ethical responsibility, in which one lives out the hard work required to have the physical tools to overcome adversity daily, not at the end of the "competition" that is life. For as Paul shows us above, daily discipline and dedication help keep us qualified for our prize, not a "super bowl" at the end of life to achieve ultimate glory.

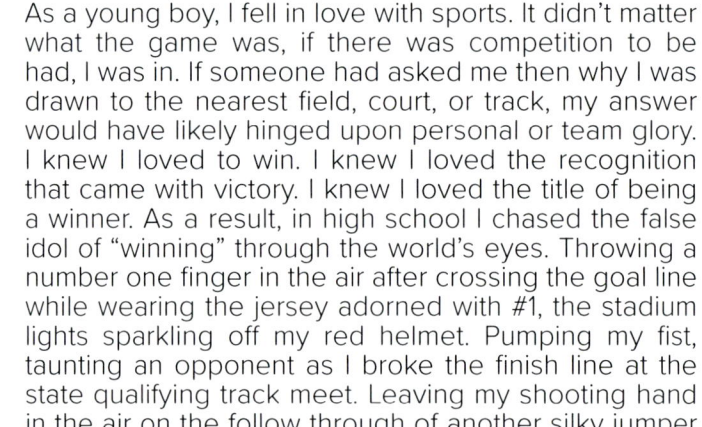

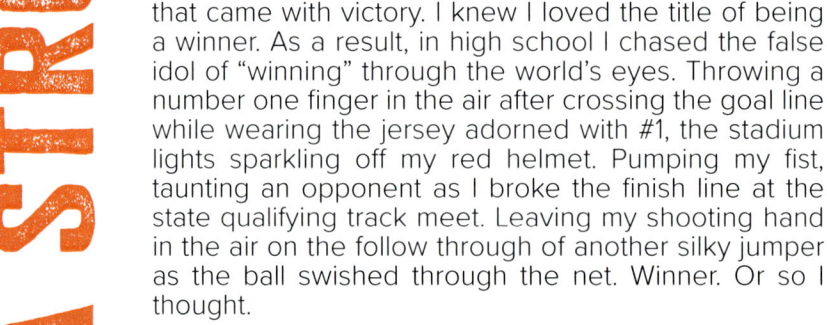

As a young boy, I fell in love with sports. It didn't matter what the game was, if there was competition to be had, I was in. If someone had asked me then why I was drawn to the nearest field, court, or track, my answer would have likely hinged upon personal or team glory. I knew I loved to win. I knew I loved the recognition that came with victory. I knew I loved the title of being a winner. As a result, in high school I chased the false idol of "winning" through the world's eyes. Throwing a number one finger in the air after crossing the goal line while wearing the jersey adorned with #1, the stadium lights sparkling off my red helmet. Pumping my fist, taunting an opponent as I broke the finish line at the state qualifying track meet. Leaving my shooting hand in the air on the follow through of another silky jumper as the ball swished through the net. Winner. Or so I thought.

I believed I was winning. And I wanted people to know it and recognize me for it. My dedication to preparation for the competitions was driven by the pursuit of victory on the scoreboard, notoriety in the headlines, or personal accolades at the end of a season. If you asked my teammates if I was someone they wanted to have next to them on gameday, they would've likely said yes because they had been fooled just like me. Tricked into believing that success was measured by the end result.

I was fortunate enough to have an opportunity to pursue athletics at the collegiate level. And true to my boyish mindset, I decided to pursue the sport that would likely afford me more opportunities at "winning." While on a recruiting trip at a small college, I was waiting to meet with the basketball coaching staff. As I stood in the auditorium looking at the trophy cases, a man in a motorized wheelchair approached me. It appeared he could only move his neck and arms slightly. He asked if I was there for the football recruiting meeting. I was caught off guard. I hadn't considered playing football in college, as per my current definition of the word, I had "lost" the most in that arena of sport. I told him I was not. He asked if I played football. I told him I did but wasn't sure I was good enough to be on a college team and playing was a priority. Without hesitation he said, "Maybe you are, and if you aren't today, what an amazing journey it will be." I didn't know what to say. He invited me to the football recruiting presentation. I agreed to attend.

After leaving the basketball recruiting session underwhelmed, I slid into a back row seat of the football meeting. A few minutes later an elderly man with a distinct limp sauntered into the room. He opened with a toothy smile that lit up the room and told us all to call him "Frosty." He walked up to each of us and shook our hand, locking in eye contact, and addressing us by our first names. He then spent the next hour presenting to us using an ancient chalk board to illustrate his points. Football was not mentioned once.

He talked about principles that I had never heard associated with sports, especially a violent game like football. He told stories about players from the program who were servants to their teammates, communities, and families. Grace and humility woven into a game based upon hitting others as hard as possible. He introduced us to the assistant coach in the motorized wheelchair name "Nellie" who was born with a rare birth defect that limited his physical capabilities from the neck down. Nellie was the team's life coach and relied almost exclusively on the players for daily care. He concluded by making us a promise that if we decided to become a part of their football family, then we would leave as winners...not on the field, but off it. There was something different about Frosty, Nellie, and this program. I didn't know what it was, but I wanted to be a part of it.

I shared my experience with my parents and told them I had to play football for Frosty (much to my mother's dismay). I then spent the next nine years of my life with the program (playing and then coaching for four years). My first impression had been correct. Frosty's team was indeed different. It was different because Frosty and his staff took boys and led them to become young Christian men. He took biblical principles and applied them to the

ATHLETE

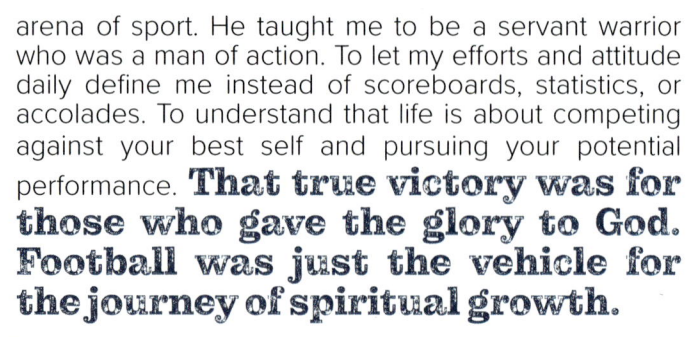

# FROM A STRONGER MAN

arena of sport. He taught me to be a servant warrior who was a man of action. To let my efforts and attitude daily define me instead of scoreboards, statistics, or accolades. To understand that life is about competing against your best self and pursuing your potential performance. **That true victory was for those who gave the glory to God. Football was just the vehicle for the journey of spiritual growth.**

As a father, son, brother, and man today, I measure winning through my promise to myself, my family, and the Lord that I will be disciplined daily in my ethical responsibilities to "strike a blow" to my body and suffer physically so that I can "win" when God calls upon me to do so. We were blessed with a physical body, and as a stronger man in Christ, you are called to a disciplined journey of maximizing your physical tools so you can serve others on "game day." You are an athlete. Your game day could be tomorrow, pulling your family from a car after an unexpected accident, warding off an unexpected assailant in the parking lot of the grocery store, playing catch with your son in the back yard, or pushing your mom's wheelchair because your dad has gone to be with Jesus. Stronger men are all called to be athletes for life's challenges, spiritually and physically. It's never too late to begin the daily journey of spiritual and physical fitness. Get after it.

## Brent, 39

"To live a disciplined life, and to accept the result of that discipline as the will of God —that is the mark of a man."

— Tom Landry

# REFLECT & DISCUSS

1. What is your biggest takeaway from this chapter? From the testimony?

2. Would you consider yourself more of a naturally disciplined or undisciplined person? When and how did you learn the value of personal discipline?

3. How are you caring for your body and physical health as an act of healthy self-leadership? What do you need to do to grow and improve in this area?

4. In which areas of life is it easier for you to be disciplined? In which areas is it more difficult? Why do you think that is? Where do you need to grow in discipline currently?

5. Which of the 6 KEY PERSPECTIVES stands out most to you and why?

_____
_____
_____

6. "*Discipline is the price of freedom and freedom is the reward of discipline.*" Where have you experienced this truth/principle in your life? What is something that comes easier or more freely for you *now* that took a lot of discipline and practice?

_____
_____
_____

7. Discuss the difference in perspective that the C.S. Lewis and Thomas Chalmers quotes give us with regard to discipline and the role of desire. Do you tend to think of your fleshly desires as strong or weak? How effective are you at telling yourself "no?"

_____
_____
_____

# TAKE ACTION

- Make note of when you say "no" to yourself this week. What helped you in those moments? What were you saying "yes" to in those moments instead?

- Write yourself a new physical training plan this week. What should it include? How often? When will you start? What's your goal? Who will help you succeed? Lead the way!

# WEEK 7

## IT'S A TEAM SPORT

For by the grace given me I say to every one of you: Do not think of yourself more highly than you ought, but rather think of yourself with sober judgment, in accordance with the faith God has distributed to each of you. For just as each of us has one body with many members, and these members do not all have the same function, so in Christ we, though many, form

# ONE BODY, AND EACH MEMBER BELONGS TO ALL THE OTHERS.

We have different gifts, according to the grace given to each of us.

ROMANS 12:3-8

## Christianity is a team sport.

I've said that phrase hundreds of times speaking to groups of men over the years. Everywhere we look in the Bible we see the powerful role, blessing, and necessity of brothers, friends, partners, co-laborers, families, tribes, fellow disciples, community—TEAMS.

All through the New Testament, we see Jesus and His team, the disciples. It's Peter, James, and John. Then later in Acts, it's Paul & Barnabas. And Luke and Timothy and Silas and Mark. Then Timothy, Titus, and some lesser-known ballers like Epaphras and Epaphroditus (talk about unsung heroes, those dudes could play—check their stats in Philippians 2:19-30 and Colossians 1:7; 4:12).

Almost every New Testament letter starts and ends with the names of gospel teammates.

Furthermore, we read in Romans 12:3-8 that the Church is itself a "gifted Body." Sounds like an athlete to me.

It's one body with many parts, with individuals making specific contributions that strengthen unified objectives. Sounds like a team to me.

I'll say it again, Christianity is a team sport.

## HOW DO YOU GET ON THE TEAM?

The answer to that question is what we call the good news of the gospel. And it's thrilling and humbling, all at once.

Technically, it starts over your head and above your paygrade. The Owner makes a call and initiates a trade. You're drafted, picked, chosen, acquired (Ephesians 1:4-6). The phone rings. You're called up. That's right, it's a bit mind-blowing and mysterious, but you didn't first choose Him—He first chose you (John 15:16). Sometimes, you connect those dots further down the road. (Q: Did you find Jesus or did Jesus find you? A: YES.)

As you hear the words of the gospel call, you suddenly or slowly (it can happen both ways) realize you don't belong on that old team anymore. You recognize you were a loser on the losing team. And that always stings a little. But as a sinner, which we all are, Satan was kicking your butt and you didn't even realize it (see Ephesians 2:1-3). But now, you start to think and feel different. You start having new thoughts and new desires. You even know you shouldn't look at the cheerleaders the same way anymore. And you don't want to (Job 31:1).

When you join the New Team, you take off the old jersey (Ephesians 4:22-24), clean out your old locker, get on a different bus, and realize you're not supposed to run the old plays anymore (1 Peter 4:1-4). You accept your new Coach (John 1:12), meet your new Teammates and crack open your new Playbook. Time to study!

Officially, a legal transaction has taken place and your identity has truly changed (Romans 8:1-4). You are a new player on a new team.

It can all be a whirlwind as you realize what has happened and what is happening. It's simultaneously liberating and scary. For a fleeting moment, you might fear you're going to miss the old team or old locker room, but that soon passes. You realize you just got a major upgrade and are a part of a perennially winning organization. In fact, you'd love for all your old teammates to be able to join you on your new team.

The old is gone, the new has come (2 Corinthians 5:17)!

Take off the old, put on the new (Ephesians 4:22-24; Colossians 3:5-14).

Welcome to Team Jesus!

## MORE ABOUT LIFE ON TEAM JESUS

Be advised, rogue prima donnas stand out all the more here and we remind each other that there is already an MVP on this team—and it ain't you or me (Phil. 2:1-11). On this team, we don't think more highly of ourselves than we ought. We think of ourselves with sober judgment, knowing there's always room to grow and improve and always things to learn from each other along the way.

All of this is the good news of God's amazing grace and the life-changing power of the gospel. Through Jesus, you get a new identity, and you get a new team. And remember, no matter the setbacks, fumbles, injuries, sacks, or losses on plays, in the end, WE WIN (1 Corinthians 15:54-57)!

*Is this getting you excited? Fueling any gratitude? Igniting any fist pumps or the need to high five someone? It's ok, that too is common.*

It is really, really, good news. Never forget, even though it's a deeply personal and individual experience, it's always a team sport. The writer of Hebrews encouraged his teammates this way:

> *See to it, brothers, that none of you has a sinful, unbelieving heart that turns away from the living God. But encourage one another daily, as long as it is called Today, so that none of you may be hardened by sin's deceitfulness. We have come to share in Christ if we hold firmly till the end the confidence we had at first.*
>
> **Hebrews 3:12-14**

## Brothers, we need a team, we need teammates, and we need to huddle up often.

"Huddle up!" Man, those are great words.

On Team Jesus, in that huddle, every man is called to become a stronger man, run with stronger men, build up stronger men, and honor stronger men among us.

Let's be clear: we are individually responsible for our personal relationship with Jesus —the reality and genuineness of our faith. But we do not make it through the obstacle course of life or advance the mission of God solo. The greatest victories and the highest highs are shared with a team. And pity the man who falls and has no one to help him up.

*Two are better than one, because they have a good return for their work: If one falls down, his friend can help him up. But pity the man who falls and has no one to help him up!...Though one may be overpowered, two can defend themselves. A cord of three strands is not quickly broken.* **Ecclesiastes 4:9-10, 12**

One of my life's core passions and pursuits is "starting fires and fanning flames for things that matter and teams that win."

I love bold vision and grand purpose. I love impact and inspiration. I love passion and teamwork. I love encouraging and inspiring others to make their best contribution. I love focused huddles, locker-room speeches, and championship teams. I love execution and winning. Especially in things that matter.

Anything less is pointless and powerless.

## WE WERE MADE FOR TEAMS

Jordan had the Bulls. Kobe had the Lakers. Brady had the Patriots.

I had the Billygoats. Not *quite* as well-known but majestic and powerful, nonetheless. Stop laughing. I love the tough, gnarly, Great Northern Railway mascot, the high mountain billygoat. Vintage Pacific Northwest. Feel free to look it up. Had to give it a shout out. I welcome the mascot debate. Which one is the GOAT? Read that question again. That's funny.

Where was I? Ah yes, great teams. I love teams! I've had the privilege of being on my incredible family team, The James Gang, with my amazing wife and four awesome kids. And Team Grace City—the elders, executive team, staff, and my local church family—world class! And City Group (small group) Leaders—heroes of the local church! And my Stronger Men group. And Stronger Man Nation! I'm on some incredible teams within the one and only, team above all teams, the Church—Team Jesus.

God designed us for community. He created families and grew nations. He designed the Church to function like an interconnected and interdependent Body, made up of many parts, functioning together to grow in strength and health and accomplish great things together.

God arranges the members in His Body as He sees fit. The Spirit is poured out upon followers of Jesus individually and collectively to strengthen, encourage, and build up that Body. Whatever you do, get connected in a local church and be all-in to strengthen and build it.

## TEAM BUILDERS AND TEAM KILLERS

**Pride VS. Humility** *Do no think of yourself more highly than you ought, but rather think of yourself with sober judgment.* **Romans 12:3**

Humility is a team builder. Pride is a team killer.

I get it. You've heard that before. Well, we need to hear it every day.

Selfishness and ego abound in men, in general, and find a special concentration in sports. But when men can bring humility to the field and an honest self-assessment that is aware of areas to grow and get better—along with a fire and passion to give it your all—that kind of attitude is contagious in a way like nothing else.

A key to humility is a growing self-awareness. The gospel of Jesus Christ opens a man's eyes and humbles a man's heart so that, for the first time, he is truly able to rightly see Jesus for who He is, see himself for who he is, and see others for who they are.

A stronger man does not think of himself more highly than he ought, and he is free to think of himself with sober judgment.

The difference in men is almost always tangible, felt, and evident. There is an "air" about a person. Arrogance reeks and repels. Humility is sweet and draws in. Humility does not make you weak; it makes you great.

It is God's grace that enables a man to see himself rightly and with sober judgment. Bye, bye, Dillon Brooks. Adios, Antonio Brown. Pride must be daily put to death and humility must be continually practiced and strengthened. Nothing will build a team or tear one down quicker.

## Division VS. Unity

*For just as each of us has one body with many members, and these members do not all have the same function, so in Christ we, though many, form one body, and each member belongs to all the others.* **Romans 12:4-5**

Unity is a team builder. Division is a team killer.

"One body, many members." The implications are profound. When applied, it brings out the beauty, joy, and power of a high-functioning, highly gifted, unified team.

When these principles are embraced and embodied, so much momentum and progress is released. When you bring individual, diverse giftedness around a collective unified mission, you're bottling lightning. The best teams do it the best.

The same is true in your marriage, in your family, and in your business. The principles that fill leadership and business books and seminars are often simply just repackaged biblical basics. The principles of unity work wherever they are applied. That's the power of God's truth. It works. Even in the wrong hands.

Think of the Tower of Babel. Think of Black Lives Matter. What makes movements, even evil ones, successful? Unity. Pastor Jimmy Evans says, "*Unified non-Christians are more powerful than divided believers.*"

Which is why it's so critical that we are unified in the truth.

Where there is unity, there is power. Unity is the secret weapon of a marriage, a family, a church, a business, and a nation. Jesus said it, Abraham Lincoln applied it, and we're seeing it unfold today. A house divided will not stand.

## NOT EVEN THE LONE RANGER WAS A LONE RANGER

As I was thinking of how to bring this chapter to a close, I was tempted to reach for the cliché, "Don't be a Lone Ranger." But then it hit me. Not even the Lone Ranger was a lone ranger! He had Tonto. He had a teammate.

So, sure, be a Lone Ranger after all…'cause, it's a team sport.

Brother, let's be sober-minded. Get on Team Jesus. Become a stronger man. Run with stronger men. Build stronger men.

*And let us consider how we may spur one another on toward love and good deeds. Let us not give up meeting together, as some are in the habit of doing, but let us encourage one another—and all the more as you see the Day approaching.* **Hebrews 10:24-25**

Stronger men, huddle up!

ATHLETE

# FROM A STRONGER MAN

Hours into my first day of football camp at Pacific Lutheran University, a small college in Tacoma, WA, I knew that my life would be forever impacted. Frosty Westering, the 9th winningest coach in college football history, required popsicle breaks and had mandatory singing and skit time. As crazy as this sounds for a college football team, what I didn't know at the time was that he was ingraining in us his understanding of success, that it is not weighed by the destination at the end of the road, but it is the road itself. Every day, we can choose to enjoy the journey. A plaque sits on my desk reminding me daily, "You don't have a good day, you make it a good day." In my years at PLU, two principal cornerstones of the Christian model for competition were instilled, practiced, and lived. Today, I strive to apply these philosophies in my life as a husband, father, and leader at work.

**Total Release**—Letting go of fear, and fully trusting that God's word and power are enough to help do your best daily. It is a belief that winning is a by-product of achievement developing into excellence. (Colossians 3:17; 3:23)

**The Servant Warrior**—Modeled after Christ, genuine leadership starts with leaders who are willing to humble themselves and serve others, yet are willing to go to battle and be ferocious when needed. (1 Samuel 17:32; Acts 2:44-45)

I am filled with an enormous sense of gratitude when reflecting back on my career as an athlete. I was fortunate enough to start as running back at PLU for 4 years, and still hold a handful of records. During my time there, we won a national championship and made multiple deep playoff runs. However, despite the success we experienced on the field, I later came to realize that true success came in learning how to pursue excellence for the simple purpose of glorifying God by making the most of the gifts God had given me. As a team, that looked like this:

- Every coach and player having a keen understanding of their role.
- Every coach and player performing their specific role to their highest ability.
- Every coach and player bringing out the best in themselves and one another through the process. *As iron sharpens iron, so we sharpen one another.* **Proverbs 27:17**

Perhaps one of the most significant takeaways from my experience in the arena was being a part of something larger than myself. I encountered firsthand the incredible synergy and momentum that is created when you are a part of a highly functional team. When all players perform their job to the best of their ability and work in unison toward a common goal, it is amazing what can be accomplished. Similar to Paul's message to the Romans regarding the body of Christ: *For just as each of us has one body with many members, and these members do not all have the same function, so in Christ, we though many, form one body and each member belongs to all the others. We have different gifts, according to the grace given to each of us.* **Romans 12:4-6**

Building upon the lessons learned as an athlete, in relation to Paul's exhortation to the church to use our gifts to build up the body of Christ, I reflect on the importance of:

- All gifts come from God...be humble, yet confident in knowing my identity is in Christ.

- Understand not everyone has the same gifts, and own those He has given to you. (I was a gifted running back, but a horrid blocker. We would have lost a lot more games if they had depended on my lack of gifting as a blocker).

- **Know who I am, and what I do best—I want to use my gifting to God's glory every day to build up the team around me—starting with my wife, kids, co-workers, friends, and neighbors.**

One of my favorite quotes is from John Wooden: "*It is amazing how much can be accomplished if no one cares who gets the credit.*"

This quote embodies what it means to work selflessly toward the greatest good. The world's model says, "If you aren't number one, you're no one," and that the definition of success is found in personal accomplishments. Conversely, the philosophy of Total Release and The Servant Warrior is about dying to self daily, using your gifts for the greatest good of the body, and allowing Christ's Spirit to lead your steps every day. God is good!

# Aaron, 41

# REFLECT & DISCUSS

1. What is your biggest takeaway from this chapter? From the testimony?

2. What's the best "team" experience you've had? What's the worst? Share about the differences.

3. What has been your experience in and with the church? What makes a healthy, strong local church? What makes a sick, weak local church? [Note: The point isn't to bash the church but to humbly recognize, discuss, grow in, and commit to personally bringing the attitude and qualities that build up a local church.]

4. Who are some of the closest friends, brothers, and teammates you've had who have helped build you up in your spiritual journey?

5. What are the dangers of being rogue, independent, or isolated? How have you seen or experienced these dangers in your own life?

_____
_____
_____

6. **HUSBANDS/FATHERS** What are the benefits and blessings to your wife and children when you are surrounded by godly men and leading your family into healthy, life-giving community?

_____
_____
_____

7. Pride/Humility. Division/Unity. How have you seen these killers and builders play out in your own life, marriage, family, etc? What are some other team killers and team builders you would add to the list?

_____
_____
_____

# TAKE ACTION

- This week, text or call those men who have helped build you up in your faith over the years. Pray for them, thank God for them, and then let them know the positive impact they've made in your life.

- Are there any other men that come to your mind who you believe the Lord is leading you to specifically, personally encourage this week? This month? Ask God to show you who that is. Take a minute to pray and listen to the Lord. Make a list. Follow through.

- Is there anyone you need to confess "team killers" to? Anyone you've been rude, arrogant, short, dismissive, or divisive toward? Man up in the Spirit and follow up to apologize where needed. Practice saying the words, "*I'm sorry. I was wrong. Will you forgive me?*"

# WEEK 8

## THROW OFF EVERYTHING THAT HINDERS

Therefore, since we are surrounded by such a great cloud of witnesses, **LET US THROW OFF EVERYTHING THAT HINDERS** and the sin that so easily entangles. And let us run with perseverance the race marked out for us, fixing our eyes on Jesus, the pioneer and perfecter of faith. For the joy set before him he endured the cross, scorning its shame, and sat down at the right hand of the throne of God. Consider him who endured such opposition from sinners, so that you will not grow weary and lose heart.

**HEBREWS 12:1-3**

The writer of Hebrews has just finished leading a tour through the Bible's version of Canton, OH or Springfield, MA.

## THE CROWD: A CLOUD OF WITNESSES

Hebrews chapter 11 is the Biblical "Hall of Fame," or "Hall of Faith" some call it.

I can hear a coach taking his team through the Hall: "*Look around, boys. This is what success looks like. These are those who've played the game before you. Read the stories of what they overcame, how they ran, how they played. And gentlemen, they are watching you play. And cheering you on.*"

We should feel the gravitas of the moment. This is sacred ground. These are the greats. This is their story. And it is also our story. These are the shoulders we stand on. These are the ones who went before—who blazed the trail.

Story after story, example after example, of great men and women of faith, who are witnesses of God's power and faithfulness. Even in great suffering, they persevered. They held on. They ran hard. They didn't give up. They didn't give in.

But there's One who rises above them all.

One who is the penultimate athlete. The greatest of all.

More than Jerry West's NBA "Logo," or Michael Jordan's "Jumpman," or Walter Payton's "Man of the Year."

Jesus Christ is the "Logo" of Christianity.

The Hall winds it's way forward, getting narrower as it were, until we are standing before Him—The One Stronger Man. He's the one we fix our eyes on and pattern our game after.

## A STADIUM: SURROUNDED AND BEING CHEERED ON

Think of the times you've gone to a large stadium event. There's something about walking into a giant stadium, isn't there? There's a buzz, an energy, an awe. It's impressive.

Here in Washington State, the high school football championship games used to be called the "Kingbowl" and be played in the legendary Kingdome. In 1995-96, my senior year, they moved the games down the road to the Tacoma Dome and re-branded it the "Gridiron Classic." Eventually, in 2000, the Kingdome was torn down, and a new stadium has been built in its place.

I have a scar on my wrist from the Kingdome turf. I got it during the championship game we lost my junior year. But the time I remember most was walking in as a freshman, early in the morning on the day of the championship game, before the lights were even on. We laid down at midfield as they flipped on the lights of the Kingdome. Those old bulbs took awhile to warm up. I can close my eyes even now and picture it.

I can also remember the Promise Keepers event my dad took me to in the Kingdome in the summer of 1995—along with 65,000 men— that place resounded and reverberated with men lifting up the name of Jesus. I love that the largest event ever held at the Kingdome was 74,000 people, on May 14, 1976, just after it was completed, during a Billy Graham Crusade.

Even those events are just a small glimpse of the stadium of heaven that is surrounding and cheering us on now. The image of being surrounded by a great cloud and crowd of witnesses is a moving picture when you engage your imagination and let it sink in.

Let's be clear: we are not playing for them. We're ultimately playing for an audience of one. There's only one approval and one whose applause matter in the end. But He's brought all the players of the past with Him to cheer us on.

Gentlemen, you are in that stadium right now. You are not in the stands. You are on the field. Others have gone before you and given it their all. The stage is set. Life itself is like one electric championship game or meet. You've got one shot at it. How do you want to run? What kind of game do you want to have? What do you need to do for that to happen?

## GETTING COACHED UP

The Coach is laying out a clear gameplan for success. But He knows, like Mike Tyson famously said, "*Everyone has a plan until they get punched in the mouth.*"

You're the one running the race, fighting the fight, playing the game. When that whistle blows each day, when that bell rings, when that ball is kicked, the jump ball tipped, or the puck dropped—at that moment—you're going to be acting and reacting, real-time, to the opportunities and opposition of the game.

The Coach slowly paces the locker-room floor, reviewing things you've heard Him say many times before. But in the moments right before the game, they carry a bit more weight. The level of intensity is rising. At the same time, He wants you to have fun and play loose. He doesn't want you psyched out. But He does want you focused.

He calls for the following three-fold action, each marked by a stirring, "Let us."

# 1. Let us...THROW OFF EVERYTHING THAT HINDERS and the sin that so easily entangles.

Brother, the Lord wants you to truly play loose and run free, unencumbered by sin and all forms of soul-defeating baggage. Stronger men do not play with sin. They deal with it aggressively, putting it to death and casting it aside by the power of the cross of Jesus. Stronger men get free. Whatever it takes. Layer after layer. They receive healing from the Father and empowering joy and confidence from the Spirit.

**There are all types of sin and baggage that weigh men down and impede their ability to run. Here are a few possibilities:**

- Maybe it's a poor relationship with your dad, the lack of his blessing, or his absence in your life.
- Maybe it's choices you've made that subtly nag at you.
- Maybe it's false words of limitation that were spoken over you.
- Maybe it's guilt or shame from past sin, especially sexual sin.
- Maybe it's lies you've believed about your identity and purpose, or the lie that God doesn't care.
- Maybe it's an addiction you haven't fully shaken loose from.
- Maybe it's regret of things said and done or things unsaid and undone.

- Maybe it's doubt and suspicion that lingers in the back of your mind.
- Maybe it's fear of failure or the sense of a looming catastrophe in your future.
- Maybe it's disappointment with your job, career, or life season.
- Maybe it's the pain of grief and loss that comes in like a flood.
- Maybe it's temptation to chase the next shiny thing that comes along.
- Maybe it's the weight of the world on your shoulders as you try to control every detail of your life.
- Maybe it's unresolved conflict that lingers in the background of your thoughts.
- Maybe it's bitterness, unforgiveness, hurt, or anger that you're allowing to camp out in a corner of your heart.
- Maybe it's skepticism, cynicism, and apathy that has built up over years of "same old, same old" church routine.
- Maybe it's stubbornness and pride toward strong leadership or spiritual authority.
- Maybe it's religious legalism that is stunting the joy of the Spirit.
- Maybe it's victim mentality, the attitude of "poor me" that looks to place blame and gain sympathy.

All of these and more are COMMON arrows of the enemy, aimed at your heart. It's the stuff that makes up the baggage men carry. They form the chains that hold men back and weigh men down.

Make way and make room for some good news: **Jesus Christ came to destroy the work of the devil and set you free!**

Every one of those arrows has been defeated and can be deflected in Christ!

Freedom is not only possible but has been *purchased* and is available for those who are in Christ. Don't settle for anything less!

In Christ, and through Christ, you CAN throw off everything that hinders and the sin that so easily entangles.

## 2 Let us...RUN WITH PERSEVERANCE the race marked out for us.

We get free so that we can run free and run far. I may not be able to run as fast as others, but I'm not running their race. I'm running mine. My goal is to be able to run as fast and as free as I can, for the distance. It's fine to pace yourself. 'Cause you want to have some gas left at the end. I'm planning on running to the finish.

Even if you've come this far and feel as though you've been running with extra weight, drop the weight and keep going. Don't give up. We're not stopping until we've crossed the finish line.

I have a list that I keep on my phone. It's my pastoral/ministry "warning list." It's the list of all the pastors I've personally known who have forfeited their integrity, blown up their ministry, destroyed their marriage, dragged Jesus' reputation through the mud, fallen away from the faith, or taken their own life. It's a sobering list. It amounts to almost one a year for the last 25 years. And those are just the ones I've personally known. The list grows every year.

It may seem morbid or odd that I would keep that kind of a list. For me, it's an important warning: stay on guard! Don't go there. Don't end up on that list. Persevere to the end. No amount of money, fame, or pleasure is worth sacrificing finishing the race.

About a year after I got saved, I began to sense the Lord was calling me to pivot from my plan, which was to pursue aeronautical engineering. I had completed the heavy science and math prereqs—engineering physics, advanced chemistry, and calculus—in order to transfer to a 4-year university engineering program. But all I could think about was telling people about what Jesus had done in my life.

It was becoming clear that I was experiencing a call to preach the gospel and serve the Church as my life's vocational pursuit. I had no clue what that entailed. But it felt weighty. Based on the track record of the first 19 years of my life, from my premature perspective, it felt risky and daunting, and, dare I say, foolish of the Lord to assign me that job! I knew, left to myself, I would totally screw it up. Another one of my life mottos is, "Apart from Jesus, I'm an idiot."

I went into the sanctuary at the church. No one was there. Only a few emergency exit signs and safety lights were on. It felt peaceful. I went to the altar at the front, knelt, and began to pour out my heart to God. I was scared. It was a trajectory-impacting moment in my life. In those days, in my naive immaturity, I was "making deals" with the Lord. I pleaded with Him, "*Lord, I don't even want to start down this road if I'm not going to finish well. I don't want to go 20, 30, or 40 years down the road and then blow it. The enemy would love nothing more than to wait until there are as many people as possible under my leadership or influence and then pull the pin on some grenade in my life and have it all come crashing down. The enemy would love nothing more than to use me to drag Your name through the mud. Don't let it happen, Lord.*" I pleaded with Him, through tears, "*Teach me the hardest lessons first and the toughest lessons early. Whatever it takes, just don't let me go 40 years down the road only to blow it.*"

I don't know how long I prayed there and wept before the Lord. Well over an hour. I was on my face, alone, in the dark. I felt the Lord tell me to take off my shoes and come closer. There was a cross at the front of the sanctuary. I took off my shoes and moved closer, kneeling at the foot of the cross. For me, this was a holy and defining moment. I don't even like writing too much about it. Because there is still a lot of time, Lord willing, on the clock. A lot of game left to play. I'm 25 years down the road from that moment. I feel it just as fresh and weighty today.

As far as I know, there are no sweating boxes of dynamite in the basement of my soul. No fuse the enemy holds waiting to light. But I'm not letting up my guard. I still sweep the basement of my soul each week. And I invite others into my life to truly know me, as well. I know I'm switching back and forth between metaphors, but I don't care. I think you're hearing me. By God's grace, I'm going to make it to the end. I'm going to run with perseverance the race marked out for me. Jesus will get all the glory. And I want that for you, too.

## 3. Let us...FIX OUR EYES ON JESUS, the Author and Perfector of our faith.

*...Who for the joy set before him endured the cross, scorning its shame, and sat down at the right hand of the throne of God. Consider him who endured such opposition from sinners, so that you will not grow weary and lose heart.* **Hebrews 12:2-3**

Nothing knocks down an athlete more than internal defeat. When you lose focus, you lose heart. Keep looking to Jesus!

The noise of the crowd, the expanse of the stadium, the hidden fears of failure all get drown out. They fade away when you focus on Your Savior.

He who began a good work in you will carry it on to completion until the day of Christ Jesus (Philippians 1:6).

My hope isn't ultimately in my legs or my strength but His. He already ran the full course for me. He faced more than I'll ever face. He endured the cross in my place and for my sin. He scorned its shame. He absorbed the wrath of God. He was rejected, mocked, beaten, spit on, crucified, pierced—dead and buried. And by enduring that, He defeated the opposition!

He saw the outcome of His race—our salvation—and joy propelled Him to run. There's no one like Jesus.

My focus should not be on myself, but on Him. If I'm overly conscious of how I'm doing, how I'm running, or what others are thinking of me, I'll get paralyzed, exhausted, discouraged, and quit. It makes me tired just writing it.

So we fix our eyes on Jesus. He already gave the perfect performance. He's authoring, and will one day perfect, our race. Our faith will be sight. Don't lose heart, brother! When you're weak and weary, He will make you strong. Fix your eyes on Jesus—the true Stronger Man!

# FROM A STRONGER MAN

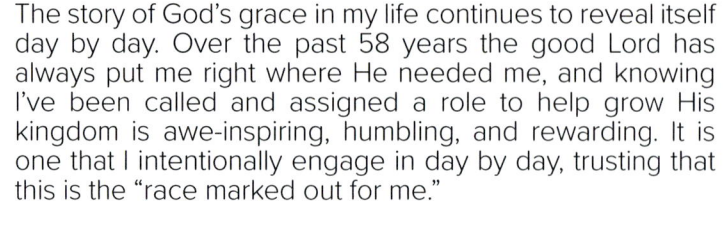

The story of God's grace in my life continues to reveal itself day by day. Over the past 58 years the good Lord has always put me right where He needed me, and knowing I've been called and assigned a role to help grow His kingdom is awe-inspiring, humbling, and rewarding. It is one that I intentionally engage in day by day, trusting that this is the "race marked out for me."

Growing up, athletics came to me quite naturally, and I loved everything about the competitions, training, and practice. I also loved the closeness that is created when you are all in and part of something bigger than yourself, like being a Christian. As a three-sport athlete in high school, football appealed to me the most. It provided me with a positive, physical outlet for my endless supply of energy, and the main source of my self-esteem. I was a jock and I wore that title proudly, not knowing at the time that sports was what I did, not who I was. I was a stand-out high school athlete and earned two scholarships to play college football at Spokane Falls Community College and Eastern Washington University. My journey to college athletics was challenging. My parents divorced when I was six. With siblings six years older than me, little supervision, and lots of free time, I was exposed to drugs and alcohol at a young age (12-13). In some ways, that normalized it in my young mind. What I thought made you a man was totally of this world, how many girls you could date, popularity, parties, and consuming drugs and alcohol. I was a lost BOY!

While athletics came easy to me, academics challenged me. Having dyslexia and ADHD, I struggled in the classroom and lacked confidence. I felt dumb. Eventually, I learned that being dyslexic doesn't mean you are dumb, but rather that you learn a different way. Throughout this time, the Lord surrounded me with many mentors to guide, push, love, and teach me to persevere. Collectively, they taught me to make the most of my God-given gifts and to endure the struggles with bad choices and secret sin that can so easily entangle. Even when my eyes were fixed on my selfish ambitions, Jesus was fixed on showing me a better way, His way!

One of my childhood mentors was my 5th/6th grade teacher, Jim Schaffner, who changed my life with father-like love and expectations. He was so much more than a teacher to me, and he never let me play the victim card. His wife, Lorene, introduced me to church and encouraged me to get baptized at age 16. In the 8th grade, Coach Taloff taught me how to be a good man through his actions and humility. I would eat lunch every day in his office with him and Coach Lesh. Many life lessons and bad jokes were learned in that office.

While my childhood dream of playing professional football was never reached, the lessons I learned along the way were preparing me for my career as a teacher and coach. These two positions have provided opportunities for me to give back to so many who made a difference in my life. As a teacher and coach, I pray every day that God will help me be intentional in the conversations I have, knowing the words I use and my interactions with my students and athletes can either build them up or break them down, encourage or discourage them. This is my 33rd year of teaching and coaching and living out His calling for me. Seeing my former students and athletes now as grown men serving others as policemen, engineers, teachers, and so many other professions is so humbling and rewarding to know I was part of the villages that helped them on their paths to becoming stronger men.

Of all the blessings I have spoken of thus far, I am most blessed to be a husband of 33 years to a woman that inspires me daily to love her, honor her, and care for her. She truly makes me want to be a stronger man. I am a father to two sons who are faithful men, husbands, and fathers. I am a grandfather to two beautiful grandsons. I am also a son, brother, uncle, friend, and above all else, a child of God. Since attending Grace City Church and being a part of Stronger Man Nation, **I have embraced the calling our Heavenly Father has given me by being in His Word daily, praying over my wife and family, and living a fruitful life. This is what gets me out of bed early every morning with a thankful heart for God's grace!**

# Doug, 59

ATHLETE

# REFLECT & DISCUSS

1. What is your biggest takeaway from this chapter? From the testimony?

2. Who are some of your all-time favorite athletes and why? What made them great in your eyes?

3. In addition to Jesus, who are some of your favorite biblical heroes and why? What's one of your favorite Bible stories?

4. In the bullet list of weights and baggage men carry, which ones most resonate with you? What sin and hindrances have you had to throw aside? How has the Lord healed you and freed you, and/or how is the Lord healing you and freeing you currently?

WEEK EIGHT

5. Early on in following Jesus, my prayer was, "*Teach me the hardest lessons first. The toughest lessons early.*" What do you think are some of the "hardest and toughest lessons" that men need to learn to persevere and finish well?

_____

_____

_____

6. What kinds and times of discouragement have you faced in your race? When have you been tempted to "lose heart" and how do you fight against discouragement?

_____

_____

_____

7. Practically speaking, how do you "fix your eyes on Jesus" each day? What does that look like and involve? How would you coach another man to fix his eyes on Jesus?

_____

_____

_____

# TAKE ACTION

- Make your own "warning list." What names come to mind of men you've seen abandon the faith and quit the race. Guard against the pride of thinking "I'm better than them" or "that could never be me." What measures do you need to put in place to help keep you from ending up on that list? What are the negative lessons those men teach you by way of warning?

- Conversely, who are the men you know who finished well? Who do you see out in front of you running a good race? Who are you watching and learning from? Pray for them to stay the course! Where possible, let them know how they encourage you.

- Lead your family in prayer this week. Attempt to make it a daily practice.

# WEEK 9

## PRESS ON TOWARD THE GOAL

Not that I have already obtained all this, or have already arrived at my goal, but I press on to take hold of that for which Christ Jesus took hold of me. Brothers, I do not consider myself yet to have taken hold of it. But one thing I do: Forgetting what is behind and straining toward what is ahead,

# I PRESS ON TOWARD THE GOAL TO WIN THE PRIZE

for which God has called me heavenward in Christ Jesus.

PHILIPPIANS 3:12-14

Paul is an example of a stronger man. A mature man. Playing the game like a champion—player and coach.

Stronger men, like Paul, have a humble assessment of the past, a firm grasp on Christ in the present, a hunger for growth, and a clear target in the future.

He's coaching us up. Like an old school coach with fire and love in his heart, he's grabbing our facemasks, securing our attention, making eye contact, and depositing wisdom, encouragement, and focus. He's preparing us to go back out on the field and keep making plays until the whistle blows.

## GRABBING THE FACEMASK

You know we've gotten soft as a culture when football coaches can no longer grab the facemask of their players. I know it has been abused and done in a demeaning and dangerous way. Those bad actors shouldn't spoil it for the rest. When I played high school football, whenever my coach grabbed my facemask, I loved it. Well, usually. Either way, I definitely needed it. It remains an image burned in my mind that defines the kind of coaching I needed, and I believe all men need, to live the Christian life and to keep going through the setbacks, missed tackles, missed blocks, dropped passes, interceptions, fumbles, trials, struggles, and battles of manhood.

There's nothing like running down a football field, full sprint, on a kickoff. As a freshman, you have no idea what you're doing. It doesn't take long before your tunnel vision has you focused on that ball carrier. You've got the perfect angle. You juke a blocker or two. You're so excited. Adrenaline is off the charts. You're about to deliver a legendary hit. When, out of nowhere, in a flash, you're upended by an upperclassman who just delivered a legendary crackback block on you. Your tunnel vision on the ball carrier suddenly became a spinning vision of your own feet in the air, swirling lights, followed by a face full of grass, and a grinning blocker standing over you. Your ears are ringing. Your body is zinging. You just got your "bell rung." Welcome to football, and manhood, son.

Side note: I know football is dangerous. Fine, make it safer. Maybe I'm just older than I realize, but crackbacks and grabbing facemasks and getting your bell rung come with the game! Know this—in the game of life, the enemy doesn't care about your safety. He's gunning for you and he's not playing fair or worried about giving you a concussion. That's what he wants to do! Like it or not, it's game on, buttercup.

You hobble toward the sideline, your teammates pat you on the back, and your coach meets you a few yards on the field. He grabs your facemask: "*James! You alright? He got you pretty good. Welcome to football, son! Now listen. James! Listen up. Look at me. Quit looking at the cheerleaders. Listen, next time, you're going to keep your head on a swivel. You'll see him coming out of the corner of your eye. I want you to turn and face him and put him on the ground! Take a breather. We'll get you back in there."*

I'm convinced that all men need that from a loving coach, brother, pastor, or friend. Often. We should hear it when we read the Bible. When you sit under good preaching. When you gather with brothers in Christ. You get knocked down, but you get back up, you get coached up, you get encouraged and built up. You learn from your experience on the field and you get back in the game more focused, more alert, more clear, and more dangerous than ever before.

Like a boxing coach in the corner between rounds. Or a football coach on the sidelines. We all need the short, punchy reminders from an outside, experienced perspective to feed us encouragement and wisdom to refocus us on the gameplan in front of us.

> **Took a punch?** *Keep moving! Keep your hands up! And watch his left jab!*
>
> **Got blindsided by the LB?** *Take a different angle next time, get low, come up under him, and knock him on his keister.*
>
> **Notice how they're playing you?** *Recognize the tactics of the enemy. He wants you to fear him. That's not going to happen. We're going to turn the tables.*
>
> **Jamming you at the line?** *I want you to jab step, swim move, and blow by him. We'll hit you down the sideline. He can't match your speed. We're going to take the fight to the opponent. Put him on his heels! Sound good? You got this.*

Knowledge. Experience. Wisdom. Faith. Encouragement. Strategy. Grit. Fire. Hustle. Self-control.

All of it can be individually tailored and personally deposited in those few moments when the lights, crowd, and distractions fade away. The eyes and voice of the coach are all that matters. Insecurity and dejection fall off you. You're reminded of who you are and what you're called to do. Confidence gets restored. Gameplan...secured. Chin strap...tightened. Mouth guard...in place. Let's do this. "Put me in, Coach!"

Knicks, bruises, scrapes, cuts, turf burns—all inconsequential. Tape the knuckles and wrists. "That's a long way from your heart." You'll be just fine.

Contact sports like football channel the ethos of stronger manhood and the Christian life. All of that, and more, is involved in following Jesus and being a man. Being a stronger man.

*"On the fields of friendly strife are sown the seeds that on other days, on other fields will bear the fruits of victory."* General Douglas MacArthur

## KEEP YOUR HEAD ON A SWIVEL

The enemy loves to deliver blindside, crackback hits. Let's consider three of them that flow from today's passage.

### BLINDSIDE #1
# PRIDE

Ah yes, the original blindside. Let's take a few more reps today exposing the tactics of pride. Here are a few of the angles pride can comes at you from:

- "Look at me" pride.
- "Poor me" pride.
- "I've arrived" pride.
- "I'm good enough" pride.
- "That's not my problem" pride.
- "I'm washed up" pride.
- "God can't use me" pride.

The enemy would love nothing more than to get you to think "I've arrived. I'm good."

This shows up in 1,001 ways in the lives of men. No one is beyond it. No one has arrived in their pursuit of humility, and no one has arrived in their fight against pride. Pride blinds you to your need for growth.

> *So, if you think you are standing firm, be careful that you don't fall!* **1 Corinthians 10:12**

> *Pride goes before destruction, a haughty spirit before a fall.* **Proverbs 16:18**

Paul shows us the mindset of a stronger man, athlete, and leader: *"Brothers, I do not consider myself yet to have taken hold of it."*

It's the mindset of the humble, hungry, teachable, hardworking, keep-training, keep-growing, keep-getting-stronger, keep-leaning-forward kind of man.

WEEK NINE

## BLINDSIDE #2
# THE PAST

The enemy loves to bring up the past. Paul specifically mentions the importance of "forgetting what is behind and straining toward what is ahead." When it comes to the past, the enemy will either attempt to use it to pull you down or puff you up. Both need to be battled and forgotten. Not forgotten in the sense that you don't cognitively remember it. But forgotten in the sense that you don't allow it to falsely define you. Forgotten in the sense that it's stripped of its power. It holds no sway over you today.

When the devil brings up thoughts of old sin and shortcomings, you lift the dumbbells of **2 Corinthians 5:17** and **Romans 8:1** and crank out a few more reps:

> *Therefore, if anyone is in Christ, he is a new creation. The old has gone, the new has come!*
>
> *Therefore, there is now no condemnation for those who are in Christ Jesus.*

When the enemy tries to puff you up through flattery of past successes, you pick up the weight of **1 Timothy 1:15** and rep it out:

> *Here is a trustworthy saying that deserves full acceptance: Christ Jesus came into the world to save sinners—of whom I am the worst.*

Neither past failures nor past successes define a man of God. The cross of Jesus is the root and source of our new identity.

The same is true for great athletes and leaders. If your last throw was an interception, you learn to forget about it. You've put in the practice, you've cultivated the confidence, your coach has your back, your team is with you, so you run back out on the field and execute the next drive. It's a mental discipline the great athletes develop.

If your last throw was a touchdown, you also set it aside, it's no time to coast or presume. It's time to go out there and execute the next play, the next throw. Good or bad, you can't dwell on the past. "Forget that last shot. Focus on the next one."

## BLINDSIDE #3
# DISCOURAGEMENT

Leaders press on when the tempting voice says, "Give up."

If Satan can't get you to quit, he'll get you to settle.

If he can't get you to settle, he'll get you to sin.

If he can't get you to sin, he'll get you sidetracked.

If he can't get you sidetracked, he'll get you discouraged.

If he can't get you discouraged, he'll try again.

Stronger men press on. They ignore uncomfortable feelings. Press through the hard. Press past the excuses. Press by the distractions. Press into the Lord.

You've got to win the battle in the mind, the battle in the heart, and the battle to get off your butt and get back in the game. Don't let the enemy blindside you!

## PLAY LIKE A VETERAN TODAY

Great leaders and great men, just like veteran athletes, keep learning, keep improving, keep focusing and refocusing. They don't quit. They don't panic. They get up, dust themselves off, hear the voice of the Coach, learn what they need to learn, forget what they need to forget, know what they're after, and get stronger as the game goes on.

That was Paul. Even though he was likely a hunched over, physically broken-down, increasingly frail guy from all the beatings he took, you just couldn't keep him down.

He had the heart of a champion, the heart of a mature, veteran athlete and coach. A leader of leaders.

His passion is contagious. His drive, impressive. His focus, unwavering.

Brothers, there is so much to strive for and to press on for. In Christ, the future is bright. In the meantime, it's a grind. It's a daily battle. The call is to press on.

**Tighten your chin strap, keep your head on a swivel, and let's get back in the game this week!**

*I am confident of this, that he who began a good work in you will carry it on to completion until the day of Christ Jesus.*
### Philippians 1:6

*Whatever happens, conduct yourselves in a manner worthy of the gospel of Christ. Then, whether I come and see you or only hear about you in my absence, I will know that you stand firm in one spirit, contending as one man for the faith of the gospel without being frightened in any way by those who oppose you.*
### Philippians 1:27-28

ATHLETE

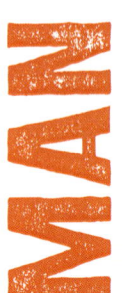

# FROM A STRONGER MAN

Sports have always been a major influence for me as far back as I can remember. God blessed me with size and athleticism that allowed me to excel in a lot of sports, but the two I enjoyed most were basketball and football. During my senior year I was recruited by a few schools for both sports and was near accepting a scholarship for football at Central Washington University. Something just didn't feel right at Central, so I chose to stay in Wenatchee and accept a scholarship to play basketball at Wenatchee Valley College.

It took years for me to recognize how much God was at work in that decision, and how staying in the valley for two more years would impact the trajectory of the rest of my life. Two major "wins" were that it allowed me to further develop and nurture my relationship with my then girlfriend (now amazing wife) and it introduced me to Adam James. Adam and I played basketball together at WVC (actually, I played, and he watched—Ha!).

**After returning to the valley 15 years later, Adam and I lived a ton of life together in a small group, and he was instrumental in demonstrating what it looks like to lead my wife and kids as a godly man. Before that, I was a bench-warming Christian settling for just attending church on Sundays. Now, I'm on the court leading for Team Jesus!** Here are three things that encourage and motivate me while on the physical court or, more importantly, while leading for Jesus on His court.

First, you play to win the game! One of my favorite quotes in all of sports comes from Herm Edwards. "YOU PLAY TO WIN THE GAME!" Over the years this quote has been parodied as comic relief; however, the point Mr. Edwards makes is profound. If you enter any sort of game with even an inkling of doubt, you've lost before it begins. I can't recall when this concept first landed on me, but it's on fire in me now whether I'm playing a pick-up game or a silly game of throwing rocks into a bucket with some friends. I use the concept even more now in my faith journey. As I follow Jesus, the confidence and certainty in knowing that Jesus wins gives me a righteous pride and motivation to keep fighting until the final buzzer—whenever our Heavenly Father decides to call me home.

**Philippians 3:12-14** says, *Not that I have already obtained all this, or have already arrived at my goal, but I press on to take hold of that for which Christ Jesus took hold of me. Brothers and sisters, I do not consider myself yet to have taken hold of it. But one thing I do: Forgetting what is behind and straining toward what is ahead, I press on toward the goal to win the prize for which God has called me heavenward in Christ Jesus.* Play to win the game, men, with all you have. And know that in the end...WE WIN!

Second, move on from the mistake and focus on the next shot. I've had the privilege to step into coaching as my sons have picked up sports. One of the hardest things to teach kids is to forget about the missed shot or bad play. It's a common reaction and something that takes a lot of coaching and encouragement to break. In the same light, we as believers tend to be hard on ourselves as we reflect on past sin and/or dwell on current sin. Please don't take this as me instructing you to not have remorse for sin, that's not what I'm saying here. However, God doesn't want us to stay there (2 Corinthians 5:17). Thanks to Jesus' sacrifice on the cross, we have redemption, through forgiveness, as we repent. Recognize the mistake, learn from it, and get your focus back on the next play.

Third, you have a chance if there is time on the clock. I've been fortunate enough to hit a few game-winners in my day. There are few greater rushes than having it all be on your shoulders to either win or lose the game for your team. One mindset that helped me be somewhat successful is that I always believe we have a chance to win right up until the final buzzer. The same goes for my mindset when pursuing non-believers. I always have the belief that God will work in His time, and there is always hope right up until the buzzer sounds. Don't shy away from taking the shot, and trust that in His timing lives can change. Except in this arena all the glory is His!

Being a leader on your sports team or as a coach can be rewarding and is a big deal. However, leading for Team Jesus is an absolute privilege, rush, and honor that far surpasses any sporting venture. It's changed my life and I pray that you don't miss the opportunity when it presents itself because I guarantee it will change yours.

# Ka'ala, 45

ATHLETE

# REFLECT & DISCUSS

1. What is your biggest takeaway from this chapter? From the testimony?

2. Who was your favorite coach who impacted you growing up? What makes an effective, empowering, great coach

3. When did you need to "press on" in life? Is there a time when you were "knocked down" and had to get up and keep going, forgetting what was behind? What comes to your mind? What helped and encouraged you in that season?

4. Discuss the blindside of pride. Do you tend to retreat toward the arrogant side or pity side of pride? What, specifically, has helped you battle these forms of pride the most?

5. Discuss the blindside of the past. How are you tempted to be puffed up by your successes or pulled down by your failures? What does the voice of the enemy sound like most often in your inner battle dialogue? What does Jesus say instead?

6. Discuss the blindside of discouragement. How have you faced and battled discouragement? What verses or passages of Scripture has God used to lift you up the most?

7. When you look ahead to, Lord willing, the next 10 years of your life, what gets you most excited? What would you like to see happening in the life of your family? Your children and grandchildren?

# TAKE ACTION

- Time for a session at the campfire—on your own, with your son(s), and/or with a group of men.

- Individually, make a list of all the past failures, mistakes, and sins the enemy tries to throw in your face and the lies the enemy has told you over the years. Write down the things the enemy says to you in the inner battle dialogue. Additionally, what things do you want/need to leave behind? These could be idols, regrets, fears, bad habits, etc. Spend an evening this week or this month sitting by a fire and thanking Jesus for your new identity in Him. When you're ready, throw the list in and watch it burn. What does the Lord say to you in that moment?

- Now write or journal a list of the truths and promises you want to carry with you as you press on in Christ. Keep it somewhere you can remember and review it, like your Bible or journal. What was that experience like?

# WEEK 10

## PREPARE YOUR MINDS FOR ACTION

**THEREFORE, PREPARE YOUR MINDS FOR ACTION;** be self-controlled; set your hope fully on the grace to be given you when Jesus Christ is revealed. As obedient children, do not conform to the evil desires you had when you lived in ignorance. But just as he who called you is holy, so be holy in all you do.

1 PETER 1:13-15

There are few things in life like game day.

When the day of the game arrives, you wake up feeling the anticipation. The opportunity. Sometimes the pressure. But there's no escaping, it's game day. It can be exciting and nerve-racking, all at once. The hours and minutes are going to melt away and there'll be no more waiting.

I remember thinking through the plan for the day. What time was I going to eat? What time was I going to head to the school/field/gym to get ready? How would I spend those few hours after school? How would I perform that night?

I remember sitting in the locker room before the game. In the fall, it was football. In the winter, it was basketball. I loved both. Both came with adrenaline. Both came with pressure. Both came with expectation. All the practice led to this. This is not a drill. This will go on our record. This one counts. Our dream of making the playoffs and winning a state championship was on the table each week, each game.

The bleachers will have fans. The pep band will be playing. The environment will be electric. Friday night lights on the small-town field with the whole town out to watch. Or a packed gym, standing room only, with heat waves rippling across the court. The opponent would love nothing more than to come in here and steal a win on our home turf.

We weren't about to let that happen.

Before a ball was kicked or tipped, the game was already well underway. The mental game. You had to be mentally locked in, mentally ready.

## "Prepare you minds for action."

Each of my teammates had his own routine. Some were light and jovial and bouncing around with energy, slapping others on the shoulder. Some were quiet, serious, focused, not to be bothered. Whatever you needed to do to get locked in, that was the assignment.

As you begin to imagine the whistle blowing and the game starting, you visualize your contribution. Offense. Defense. Taking shots. Making a cut. Breaking down and making a tackle. Delivering a hit. Catching a pass. Jumping for a rebound. I've made a lot of 3-pointers in my mind's eye. I've hit game-winner after game-winner—in my mind's eye. Caught touchdown pass after touchdown pass. Juked defender after defender. Some of it translated to reality. All of it was part of the process—of the way you prepare—to compete and play your best when it mattered.

Even in my small-time experiences, I saw the reality of the difference between those who had mental toughness and the ability to channel their thoughts and emotions to play their best when it counted most, and those who didn't. In some cases, there were those who had more raw physical talent but were mentally weak, let the nerves get to them, or simply got accustomed to losing and ended up underachieving. It reminds me of the saying, "*It's not the size of the dog in the fight, but the size of the fight in the dog.*" Although, at some point, let's be honest, the size of the dog matters. Still, when put up against peers, mental toughness is a game-changer.

Legendary college basketball coach John Wooden architected the "pyramid of success." These are 5 levels of essential attributes required to reach the pinnacle that he dubbed, "competitive greatness." The base layer had 5 qualities: industriousness, friendship, loyalty, cooperation, enthusiasm. The next layer had 4 more: self-control, alertness, initiative, intentness. Then 3: condition, skill, team spirit. Followed by poise and confidence. And topped off with "competitive greatness."

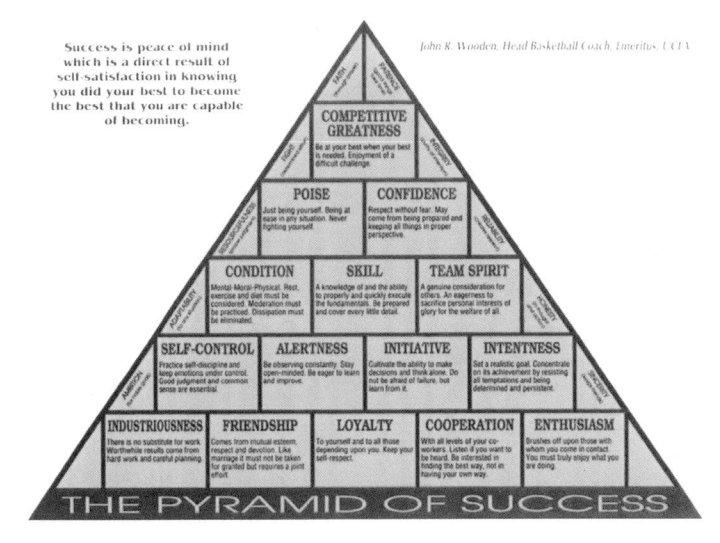

Wooden defined competitive greatness as follows: **"Be at your best when your best is needed. Love the hard battle."**

Being at your best when your best is needed involves all the training, practice, physical preparation, and mental preparation you can muster. And you know what? Even though I'm not lacing up cleats or tearing off warmups anymore, those same qualities and attributes that propel any athlete to his or her best personal performance in a game all carry over to my role as a man endeavoring to be a faithful and loving husband, a present and empowering father, a focused and impactful leader, a builder and encourager of men, and above all, a passionate and devoted follower of Jesus Christ.

## Holiness matters. Excellence of character matters. Faithful reputation matters.

When you see the pursuit of stronger manhood through the lens of the athlete and leader, you realize the real game has much higher stakes and is worth far more than a high school trophy, college scholarship, or tryout for the big leagues.

Being a husband IS the big leagues. Being a dad IS the big leagues. Being a Christian IS the championship game of life.

Men, we do need to step up. Think hard. Put in the hours. Stay up late. Get up early. Mentally prepare, live with self-control, pursue righteousness and holiness, and take the field with confidence and fire in our eyes.

I will advocate for that kind of life pursuit for all men till the day I die. There's just too much at stake! And it's the life we were created to live—the fight we fight, the game we play, the race we run.

And to be honest, I praise God that all of those years and experiences growing up playing sports were just the appetizer for the life of leadership as a man. With this perspective, the thrill is far from gone when sports end. Life is truly an incredible journey and a total gametime adventure!

Anyone who has played a sport knows there's sadness when it's over. But if it's the thrill of the game you're seeking, if it's the thrill of the championship run and the heart-beating anticipation—the Christian life is for you. Following Jesus is the pure origin of those experiences. He's calling you to greatness. He's calling you to give it your all. He's calling you to go all in. Mind. Heart. Body. Soul.

Let me address a constant danger in being misunderstood. The Christian life in one grand and glorious sense is not ultimately about your "performance."

You don't score your way to heaven. You don't save yourself. You can't. You don't have to clear the bar to be saved. You can't. The bar is way too high. You couldn't jump that high in your prime.

**Only one Man gave the winning performance,** the true Victor and ultimate Champion, Jesus Christ. His performance and His victory were imputed—given, applied—to you through your repentance and faith in Him. He was the representative of Team God, who stepped onto the field and emerged victorious, and that victory extends to anyone and everyone who is on Team Jesus. He's the MVP, not you. Your salvation is based on His performance, not yours. That's really, really good news. So, in that sense, you can rest and receive a victory that Someone else achieved in your place.

Your identity is secure in Him. It doesn't rise or fall on your daily or weekly performance. To live under that kind of pressure is the definition of man-made religion that can only lead to pride or despair. Let's understand that and keep that really clear.

AND, yet still in another sense, God IS calling you to perform. He's calling you to live a new life of righteousness and godliness and holiness, powered by the presence of the Holy Spirit in your life.

Your obedience matters. Your faithfulness matters. Not in the sense that your salvation is hanging in the balance on a moment-by-moment basis, but the Bible says our faith and love of Jesus is proved genuine by our obedience, by the fruit—the actions and words—of our lives.

Your life can glorify God to a greater or lesser degree according to your faithfulness. Without question.

You can be a dad who is in the game, loving and leading his sons and daughters as you point them to Jesus. Or you can be a dad who is checked out, MIA, and someone your children will eventually need to "overcome."

What will make the difference? In a real way, men, your performance. Your actions. What you DO does indeed make a difference.

Salvation is by faith alone, not by works. The Christian life, however, is a life made up of good works, fueled by faith. True faith produces real action.

You are not saved by works, but you are saved for works.

So, yes, friend, every day is game day. It's game on. The clock is ticking. The ball is in your hands. It's not wrong for a man to feel that pressure. It shouldn't crush you, but it should bring you to your knees.

It shouldn't cause you to freeze and get paralyzed. It should cause you to focus and dig in.

> ***"Prepare your minds for action."***
>
> ***"Be self-controlled."***
>
> ***"Set your hope fully on the grace that will be given you when Jesus is revealed."***
>
> ***"Do not conform to the evil desires you had when you lived in ignorance."***
>
> ***"As he who called you is holy, be holy in all you do."***

Your assignment is to get mentally locked in and then take the field each day and be at your best when your best is needed.

It's game day, brother. You ready?

*WEEK TEN*

> "It's not whether you get knocked down; it's whether you get up."
>
> — Vince Lombardi

# FROM A STRONGER MAN

Growing up, I was known at church as the kid who played baseball. And to my baseball peers, I was known as the kid who went to church. My family was very religious, attending church twice on Sundays as well as a mid-week service. I was taught the Bible, that Jesus died on the cross for me, and the reality of right and wrong. I was well disciplined by my parents, which thankfully saved me from a lot of poor decisions and the associated consequences.

I remember being 6 or 7 and spending many evenings out in the backyard with my dad sitting on a bucket, glove in hand, and me standing 45 feet away. My task was to throw 100 pitches and hit the glove every time. It seemed like we did this for weeks leading up to my first little league tryout. You can imagine our disappointment when we found out that my first year of little league would be pitching machine only, and that all that effort would have to wait another year. But it was those early investments, along with thousands more hours put in by my parents and coaches over the years, to train, develop, and encourage me as a pitcher that eventually led to my winning performance in the 2005 Washington State 4A High School Baseball Championship game. Then I pitched the first perfect game in my high school's history the following year and ultimately accepted a Division I baseball scholarship to Gonzaga University.

In addition to my successes, I have experienced many devastating failures: untimely injuries; single-handedly causing my high school summer team to lose the national championship; being cut from the traveling squad and relegated to an overcompensated bench-warmer during my junior year of college. These failures are an inevitable part of athletics, and for me they challenged who I thought I was and made me question whether or not I could continue.

Very few things have revealed how mentally weak and fragile I am as much as being an athlete. My inherent response to failure is to react—in anger, foolishness, self-pity, and hopelessness. But my college pitching coach gave our pitching staff some of the best advice I've ever received for dealing with failure in real-time. He said, *"When you're pitching and you give up a big home run, everyone on the other team loves it when you react. You stomp around on the mound, throw your glove, swear and cuss, or let loose the famous 'body-wah,' like a 2-year-old who just got told 'no.' And the other team loves it. We will not do that.* **When we give up a big home run, we will RESPOND. We will not react. We will keep our composure. We will get back up on the mound. We will have our heads up and eyes focused.** *There's another batter coming, and our job is to strike him out."*

There is a biblical concept here that applies to how all stronger men need to address their failures. When your marriage is failing, when your parenting is failing, when you're failing as a leader, whenever your failure is staring you right in the face, remember the biblical call to be fully alert and sober-minded. Jesus wants His men to be serious, self-controlled, and clear as they stare down their failures. You need to refrain from that pride and panic-induced reaction; instead, you need to respond.

So how do you do that? Stop focusing on yourself and your failures. When you react in despair, you take yourself out of the game, walk off the field with your head hanging, and the enemy loves that. Instead, look to Jesus and His performance. He's loved your wife and children far better than you ever could. He's built more, fixed more, accomplished more than you could possibly dream to. He absolutely does not need you, because He is the Champion. But if He's chosen you to be on the team, it's because He wants you to get to experience the glory that awaits when He returns as the Champion and once and for all claims the final, decisive victory for His team. With that truth in mind, you can respond with confidence and courage to step into the work He has called you to. Just because you gave up a homerun doesn't mean you can't strike out the next batter. Pick up your head, focus on Jesus, and stay in the game.

# Jeremy, 35

*ATHLETE*

# REFLECT & DISCUSS

1. What is your biggest takeaway from this chapter? From the testimony?

2. How did/do you do with performing in front of people? In sports, music, public speaking, etc., do you get nervous? Excited? How did you prepare for a big game or performance?

3. How do you mentally prepare each day, or each week, to lead your family in a godly way? How do you, practically, "prepare your minds for action?"

4. Let's talk about "performance." In what ways can a focus on "performance" be a hindrance to our relationship with God? In what ways is the call to act in a godly way helpful and essential? What makes the difference between healthy and unhealthy "performance?"

5. Honestly reflecting and assessing the strengths and weaknesses of our dads is an important part of the journey of manhood and charting the course we want to run. What did your dad do or not do that was helpful and a blessing in your life? What did he do or not do that was challenging, difficult, or painful?

_____

_____

6. Where is there a need for renewed ACTION in your life and leadership currently?

_____

_____

7. The imagination is powerful. It can be healthy or unhealthy, helpful or unhelpful. Like visualizing a game winning shot. Or meditating on a verse of Scripture. How can you or do you leverage and use a sanctified imagination as a helpful tool in the mental game of the fight of faith?

_____

_____

_____

# TAKE ACTION

Prepare your mind for action. Give yourself an extra 15-30min each morning this week. Focus on a different member of your family each morning. Find a verse to use to pray for them and encourage them with (if you don't know where to look, just use the Proverb that corresponds with the day of the month). Write out a prayer for that member of your family, asking God to bless them and thanking God for them. What are strengths you see in them and attributes you appreciate? Write them down. What is an area for growth that you see that you will pray for? Write it down.

# WEEK 11

## IT'S NOT HOW YOU START; IT'S HOW YOU FINISH

I have fought the good fight, **I HAVE FINISHED THE RACE,** I have kept the faith. Now there is in store for me the crown of righteousness, which the Lord, the righteous Judge, will award to me on that day—and not only to me, but also to all who have longed for his appearing.

2 TIMOTHY 4:7-8

2 Timothy is, without question, one of my favorite books of the Bible. It's the man-making manual of the New Testament. It's home base for this Biblical Manhood Series. The Soldier, Farmer, Athlete, and Son identities are taken directly from 2 Timothy 2:1-7.

It's also Paul's last letter. He is passing the baton to his spiritual son, Timothy.

**It's a leadership succession masterclass.**

Paul knows he is near the end. In 2 Timothy 4:6, he says, "*The time for my departure has come*." As he nears the end of his life, he has the testimony every stronger man wants at the end. He is finishing well.

He's come a long way, hasn't he? Yet he can confidently say, "*I have fought the good fight, I have finished the race, I have kept the faith*."

Remember where Paul started? Murdering Christians!

Brothers, there's perhaps no greater example of this truth: it's not how you start, it's how you finish.

## THE KENTUCKY DERBY

I watch one horse race a year. The Kentucky Derby. It always falls on the same day as our town's community festival main event—the Apple Blossom Grand Parade. We have some good friends that are really into horse racing. They follow it all year long. They know the owners and trainers and history. One year, after watching the parade together, we planned to host a BBQ afterward and they said, "Only if we can watch the Derby." Sure, I thought. I'm a sports guy. Sounds great.

Now, mind you, there are hours of coverage leading up to the actual race. Interviews and documentaries on favored horses or famous owners. The outfits, the hats, the infield, the festivities. I was blown away. Sure, I had heard of the Kentucky Derby, but oh man! Apparently, it's a really, really big deal to some. Bigger than I'd realized. But still, I honestly thought, "*All of this, for a 2-minute horse race??!!*"

Talk about media and marketing getting their bang for their buck. Hours of coverage, millions and millions of dollars, for a 2-minute race. Wild!

Come to find out, they call it "the most exciting 2 minutes in sports." And I can honestly say now...I agree! I'm hooked! It's incredible every year.

Each year, I make a blind guess to pick my favorite to root for. It's fun to see which horse names people like the best. And once you have your horse picked, the race is even more electric. I can never sit through it. I end up on my feet, shouting at the TV and taking it all in.

# WEEK ELEVEN

Here's where all of this is going: do yourself a favor and look up the video of the 2022 Kentucky Derby.

I haven't been able to watch it once without tearing up, and I've watched it many, many times. In fact, whenever I'm feeling a little down or tired or discouraged, I pull it up and watch it again. It delivers every time.

**Go ahead. I dare you to pull it up and watch it right now. I'll wait.**

If not, that's fine, but I'm about to spoil it for you. But it's so good it won't matter. It still won't actually spoil it for you.

In 2022, a horse named "Rich Strike," the longest shot, won the Kentucky Derby.

I say again: the longest shot. As in, 80-1 odds. And only 20 horses run the race!

He's so far back for most of the race that the announcer only briefly mentions his name early in the race when he rattles off the names of all the horses. And you don't hear "Rich Strike" again until literally the final seconds of the race.

Other horses are neck-and-neck in the lead. Back and forth, their names are called. It's a blazing fast first and second quarter of the 1.25-mile race.

The most heart-pounding moment every year for me is the great announcement when they make the final turn. "AND DOWN THE STRETCH THEY COME!!"

As someone who used to dream of being a sports announcer—Oh, man!—it's an incredible moment.

The final stretch. Now is the time to be glued to the screen. Pay attention! This is it! Everything is decided in the final stretch. The jockeys are spurring their horses on. Every muscle in every horse is firing full speed. This is the first time these 3-year-old thoroughbreds have ever run this distance. Who will it be??

I can't stay seated.

In the final stretch of the 2022 Kentucky Derby, Rich Strike, again—the longest shot, at 80-1—comes from the back, weaves through traffic, ducks to the inside position, pushing, straining, gaining, running. Past one horse. Then another! And another!! Yet still, the announcer, the incredible Larry Collmus, pays him no attention until the final glorious call.

Shockingly, Rich Strike appears in the final seconds, charging past the other two horses in the lead, who are essentially the only names you've been hearing on the back stretch.

I close my eyes and picture someone tuned in to the radio who can only hear the race being called. Someone who can't see the red and white jockey plowing ahead on the inside. Suddenly, Larry Collmus makes the now famous call: "RICH STRIKE! IS COMING UP ON THE INSIDE—OH MY GOODNESS—THE LONGEST SHOT HAS WON THE KENTUCKY DERBY! RICH STRIKE HAS DONE IT IN A STUNNING, UNBELIEVABLE UPSET!"

Rich Strike??!! Where'd he come from?! It's absolutely incredible.

One of the greatest come-from-behind victories in Derby history. Many call it one of the greatest "calls" in sports announcing history. The energy and inflection in his voice. The excitement and exclamation with the perfect choice of words for maximum impact on the viewer and listener.

THAT, friends, is how you finish a race. And how I imagine heaven announcing Paul's finish. And, Lord willing, yours and mine.

I'm guessing there might be a few men reading this who would honestly agree, they didn't have the best start to their race in life and in faith.

You may even feel like you're down. Like you're behind. Like you're a long shot.

Friend, you may be down, but you're not out. The race isn't over. You can still finish strong.

## WHAT IS FINISHING STRONG? KEEPING THE FAITH.

From this point forward, run after Jesus. Live with integrity. Live for Him. Don't hold back. Fight. Run. Keep the faith. Finish.

What awaits you is incredible—the crown of righteousness.

Jesus himself will hand it to you. The LORD. The righteous Judge will give YOU the crown of righteousness. Mind-blowing. Those listening to that play-by-play call on the radio will jump out of their seat. Adam James?! Where did he come from?! The crown of righteousness?? That guy??

It's amazing grace. Paul, the Christian-killing, Jesus-persecuting, self-righteous pharisee of pharisees, receives the crown of RIGHTEOUSNESS?!

Yep. And not only Paul. "All who have longed for His (Jesus') appearing."

## HOW OFTEN DO YOU THINK ABOUT "THE END?"

What will those final moments of your life be like?

None of us can ever really know when or how it will go down. But it's good to imagine ourselves running hard, loving Jesus more than we ever have, down the stretch. And since we don't actually know when that will be, maybe that's how we should live every day.

We should look forward to the finish. We should never lose hope. We should long for His appearing. Do you?

In recent years, it makes even more of an impact on me. With all the chaos in the world, it's clear to see why the prayer of the saints—the final prayer at the very end of the Bible—on the last page, in the last chapter, is, "Come, Lord Jesus."

Brothers, the name of the game is not how you start but how you finish.

The name of the game is to run for the crown. Finish strong. And long for His coming. Glory awaits.

Run for the crown. Long for His coming.

In the meantime, Paul tells Timothy to do 4 things in the verses just before:

## 1. Keep your head in all situations.
## 2. Endure hardship.
## 3. Do the work of an evangelist.
## 4. Discharge all the duties of your ministry.

You might be tempted to think that is just for pastors—from an old pastor to a young paster. And that's true, in part. But it's written for all Christians. Certainly, all Christian men. A masterclass.

Keep your head in all situations. Endure hardship. Do the work of an evangelist—which is simply being faithful to tell others about Jesus. And discharge all the duties of your ministry. In other words, before you die, make sure you empty your clip. Whatever bullets the Lord has given you to fire—whatever gifts, influence, leadership, opportunities—use it all. Leave it all on the field.

Men, let's spur one another on to the finish.

And when the call is made—"DOWN THE STRETCH THEY COME!"—Keep kicking hard.

When you do, you'll inspire the next generation to do the same. And the seed of a legacy of strong finishes will be firmly planted. Generation to generation. Passing the baton in the race of faith.

May your latter years be more victorious than your former. Keep the faith! Finish strong!

*WEEK ELEVEN*

> "The secret of my success over the 400 meters is that I run the first 200 meters as hard as I can. Then, for the second 200 meters, with God's help, I run harder."
>
> — Eric Liddell

ATHLETE

# FROM A STRONGER MAN

Anyone who knows me is aware I am a baseball lifer. I was introduced to baseball by my maternal grandfather. As an infant, I was taken to Candlestick Park for a Giants game and around age 7, to Metropolitan Stadium to watch the Twins and Yankees. Beginning at age 9, with the help of my "Big Brother," Ray Kimmel (who was provided through the Big Brother Association in Spokane), I have taken every opportunity to be involved in the game at some level. But as Jim George famously said, "It's not how you start that's important, it's how you finish!"

As a left-handed pitcher that could throw hard, throw strikes, and make hitters look silly, I was comfortable in the center of the diamond with all eyes on me. I honed my skills and continued my baseball career in college, having much success, both individually and as part of a team. Due to a series of elbow injuries which began at age 15, I went undrafted, and had to figure out how to keep baseball as a part of my future. My baseball career had started well, but I thought it was ending poorly, and by age 21, I was pretty sure I was done.

While in college, my primary catcher, Kirk Acey, a fellow brother in Christ, took me under his wing my senior year and discipled me. Together, we conducted Bible studies in our hotel rooms before Sunday road games. He really showed me how a young man can live the Christian life and thus I feel I had a good start in my walk with Jesus.

As a boy and then young man growing up in a single-parent home for most of my childhood, I didn't have a godly father to show me what it looked like to honor God, cherish your wife, raise your kids, and serve the Lord. As I reflect, however, God had, and continues to provide godly men that have shown me these things. They were friends, coaches, teachers, professors, pastors, elders, etc. Many of these men have or are now finishing their lives here on earth well. They have fought the good fight; they have finished the race, they are keeping the faith, and they eagerly await the crown of righteousness, which the Lord, the Righteous Judge, will award them on that day.

*WEEK ELEVEN*

My wife, Susan, and I have three adult children; two sons love and serve the Lord. Our daughter professed Christ as a teen, but has since told us she doesn't have a personal relationship with Christ. We pray for her, her husband, and our two grandchildren all the time. We realize that we may start a race (teaching our kids about Jesus), but often the Lord has other plans for now and for how it may end. The key is finishing well: being faithful to live and proclaim the Word, being humble, and leaving the results to the Lord. We pray we may see her family come to saving faith while we are still here on earth.

As for baseball, like so many athletes who can't DO anymore, I was able to move ahead into teaching and coaching. I was blessed to be a baseball coach, from T-ball age to college, for 30 years. I even coached girls' bowling for 4 years here in Wenatchee. For the past 15+ years I've been a baseball official, umpiring ages 9 up to the Wenatchee AppleSox (a collegiate summer baseball team). I get to teach others through Wenatchee Valley College who want to learn to be baseball umpires. And I continue to teach kids baseball skills, and life skills, by passing on the many things I've learned—both on the diamond and through tutoring. God is allowing me to finish well by using the gifts He's given me, by giving back to a game that has been a passion in my life.

**More importantly, I seek to fight the good fight, finish the race, keep the faith, and should Christ tarry, turn any crown I may have back to the Lord, as He deserves all the praise, honor, and glory for anything good He has done in and through me.**

# Jeff, 61

*ATHLETE*

# REFLECT & DISCUSS

1. What is your biggest takeaway from this chapter? From the testimony?

_____
_____
_____

2. What is the most exciting sporting event, moment, victory, or performance you've ever seen? What are some of the great ones that come to mind? How do these moments translate to finishing strong in the race of faith? What lessons can you glean from those moments?

_____
_____
_____

3. When you think about "finishing strong," what does that include? What would that look like to you?

_____
_____
_____

4. What do you think men need to know/be/do in order to finish strong? What must be practiced? What must be avoided?

_____
_____
_____

5. What would you include in your last letter/message to your sons/daughters? What would you emphasize? How would you encourage and instruct them?

_____
_____
_____

6. Why is it helpful to think about the end? What benefits can we gain from contemplating the end? What's good about it? What's hard about it?

_____
_____
_____

7. What are the most important things you could do this week and this month, to show and tell your family what really matters most?

_____
_____
_____

# TAKE ACTION

- Practice writing a version of a final message to your family. If you only had time to give them a Top 10 list of things to know, remember, and carry with them, what would your Top 10 be? I know that may seem morbid and odd. But it's an incredibly powerful exercise.

    *"Dear family, in case I can't be there at some point in the future, here's what I would want you to know and carry with you. Above all, know that..."*

    *"In no particular order, always remember the following: 1) ... 2) ... 3) ..."*

- Plan a time to share it with them! Why wait until you're gone to say the most important things? You can simply set it up this way—tell them, "I was given this assignment by Pastor Adam in the Athlete book to write a version of a final message to you if I only had time to give you the Top 10 things I want you to know and carry with you. I want you to hear and know my heart for the things that matter most. So that we can all endeavor to live with these in mind each and every day!"

- What was helpful about that exercise? What was hard?

# WEEK 12

**SETTLE THE GLORY ISSUE: ALL IN, ONE NAME**

Whenever the living creatures give glory, honor and thanks to him who sits on the throne and who lives for ever and ever, the twenty-four elders fall down before him who sits on the throne and worship him who lives for ever and ever.

They lay their crowns before the throne and say:

"You are worthy, our Lord and God,
to receive glory and honor and power,
for you created all things,
and by your will they were created
and have their being."

REVELATION 4:9-11

All of history is moving to a roaring moment of glory and praise to the only God and Creator of all things. Even now, songs of praise and expressions of worship flow unhindered toward His throne.

There is only One who is worthy of this praise. Every crown that can be given or won will one day be laid down before the King of kings and Lord of lords, Jesus Christ. What a scene!

One of the biggest lessons and dangers of sports is the thirst for glory. The athlete chases the crown. The champion is given a party and paraded through town. The confetti falls. Cigars and champagne pop out.

The thirst for glory is not only seen on the championship stage but after any given play or game. The human propensity to seek praise is, all too often, on full display. And it lives in every man's heart.

The rafters. The banners. The trophies. The crowns. The medals. The rings. The ring of honor. The headlines. The adoring crowds. The endless highlights. The last shot. The gleaming lights. The shuttering cameras. The pressing mics. The autographs. The posters (remember posters?).

**Sports is the arena of glory. Glory. Glory. Glory. Glory.**

Sports provide the scenery, storyline, emotions, and moments that elicit the greatest explosions of praise in our society and produce what looks and sounds like the most ardent and adoring worshippers. Victory and songs. Sports and entertainment.

There's nothing wrong with the thrill of victory—it's good and right to crown champions and cheer the winning team, yet there is a serious danger lurking, not in the dark but in the lights.

## The reality is this: God doesn't share His glory.

*I am the Lord; that is my name!*

*I will not yield my glory to another*

*or my praise to idols.*

### Isaiah 42:8

## YOU WERE MADE TO WORSHIP

Humans were made to worship, not be worshipped. There's just one problem. We're glory hogs. Because of our sin, our worship is distorted. It has shifted from the Creator to the created. This is what went wrong in the beginning. This is the essence of "sin." Idolatry.

Our worship is like Shaq's free throws...broke. But we keep on shooting 'em.

Worship from the human heart is like a garden hose stuck in the on position. It's not a question of if you are worshipping, it's just a question of what is getting wet. Where are you directing your worship, where are you aiming the garden hose of your heart?

We are all like billboards—constantly promoting something or someone. It's not a question of "if" but of "who" or "what" we're honoring.

If you want to experience the power, blessing, freedom, and joy of God in your life, and you want your life to count in the end, you have to get the glory issue settled in your heart. Early and often.

## ONE NAME: GOD'S SENSE OF HUMOR AND A CLEAR MESSAGE

My mom kept a pretty good scrapbook of my high school sports memories. I wasn't the star of the team or the best player. I was a decent role player on a good team with some great players. For a small town and small school, we had a solid group of athletes who could compete with, and often even beat, bigger schools.

On a dramatically smaller scale, you could say I was like a Robert Horry. A small-town "Big Shot Rob." I came through clutch in some key moments of big games and certainly contributed to our success. But if you're scratching your head trying to remember who Robert Horry was—well, exactly. If you follow the NBA closely, you might remember who he was. Otherwise, you're more likely to remember Hakeem Olajuwan, Shaquille O'neal, Kobe Bryant, and Tim Duncan. Those were the stars on the teams Horry played on and won championships with.

Ok, I was nothing like Robert Horry. He played in the NBA for 16 seasons and won 7 NBA championships. It's a metaphor. Roll with it!

The point: I was not the perennial all-star. So whenever I had a good game and got my picture and name in the paper, it was special. Usually, they got it right. However...

My senior year in football, I caught what ended up being the game-winning touchdown pass in the semi-final game—in the Tacoma Dome. It was 4th and long, on the opponent's 25-yardline, with a 1:46 to go in the 4th quarter. My longtime childhood friend, and our star, record-breaking quarterback, Patrick Hunter, lofted one of his passes toward the end zone. Everything felt like slow motion. I knew it was 4th down. Knew I had to catch the ball. My defender was a few steps behind.

ATHLETE

The ball hung in the air. I ran under the perfectly thrown pass and it fell into my hands near the back of the end zone. I clinched it tight and lifted it high. Right in front of the Wenatchee World photographer. I threw both hands in the air in a "V"—*click* *click* *click*. We ended up winning the game 52-50 to advance to the Championship game. The rest, as they say, is history.

The next day, on the front page of the sports section was a big picture of me with the ball in the air. The caption read:

*"James Adams reacts to what proved to be the winning touchdown for Pateros at the Tacoma Dome on Friday."*

Great job, James Adams. Great job.

Oh, but it gets better.

After completing our 12-0 championship season in football, we hit the hardwoods for basketball season. As I've already shared, we ended our senior year with a 29-1 record and the state championship title in basketball, as well.

There's a book about the history of the Washington State "B" Basketball Tournament called "Remembering the B." It's a beautiful, large, hardcover, 446-page, coffee-table size book that covers the history of the tournament from 1931 to 2010. Forever memorializing the storied history of these small-town kids with big time dreams. Think "Hoosiers," only in WA state.

On page 209, you find the write-up for the 1996 championship game. It was the first year in the new Spokane Arena—the start of a significant new chapter in State B history. My Pateros Billygoats defeated the St. George's Dragons, 77-51. Our best player, the State B player of the year, Garrett Zwar, led the way with 21 points—15 in the first quarter. After that, it was seniors Pat Hunter and "Adam Jones" who led the way.

Yep. Adam Jones. Hunter and Jones.

I had the second highest point total on our team, finishing with 19, including 11 in our runaway 30-point 4th quarter. Well, Adam Jones did.

Classic. The Seattle Times, The Spokesman Review. The Wenatchee World. All picked up and published the news of the glorious championship run and the efforts of the three seniors: Zwar, Hunter, and that "Jones" and "Adams" kid.

I can honestly say it's become a fun story and running joke of my life. How such a seemingly simple name, albeit two first names, can be botched so many times, right when it counts! It provides some good laughs for my close friends, and I don't mind playing it up and telling

WEEK TWELVE

*James Adams reacts to what proved to be the winning touchdown for Pateros at the Tacoma Dome on Friday.* World photo/Mike Bonnickse

## A perfect fit in Tacoma

■ Pateros runs dome

the stories with some animation. "*Of course! Give me a break! My one moment of glory! Can't even get my name right!*"

In reality, it was desperately needed for me then, and is still so, so good for me now. Absolutely perfect. In fact, our editing team handed me an early copy of the "Farmer" book (Book #2 in this Biblical Manhood Series) with a fake cover on it that said "Adam Jones" on the bottom.

I initially missed it, then erupted in laughter. Perfect. Well played.

### IT'S NOT ABOUT YOU OR ME

A friend and I were talking a few years back and he brought up an excellent observation. "Do you know the names of your parents?" He asked. The answer was of course, "Yes." "How about your grandparents?" Again, "Yes." "How about your great-grandparents?" It took me a few minutes to do some mental math and jog the memory, but I could come up with most of them, though not all of them. "How about your great-great-grandparents?" Silence. Nope. I'd have to dig up the family archive and refresh my memory. Maybe I had heard of them? I couldn't remember.

If you could come up with some of your great grandparents—that's not too uncommon. But a mere "two greats" in and most get fuzzy. Think about how profound that is? Just a few generations will pass, and your own descendants won't even be able to recall your name.

It's just not about you. How often do we need to remind ourselves of that?

There was a gospel quartet formed in 1960 called The Williams Brothers. They wrote a song called "I'm Just a Nobody." And the main lyric of the song says, *"I'm just a nobody trying to tell everybody, about somebody who can save anybody."*

That is the truth. And it must get down in the bones of all stronger men.

A reporter once asked Billy Graham what it was like seeing his name on the marquee board over Madison Square Garden, and he responded by saying something to the effect of, *It terrifies me, because God doesn't share His glory with anyone*.

In the end, your name and my name will not be remembered and will not matter. There's only one name that matters in the end. Only one name worthy of printing and remembering and exalting.

## YOUR NAME AND RENOWN ARE THE DESIRE OF OUR SOULS

I've grown up and been greatly impacted over the last 25+ years by the ministry of Louie Giglio and Passion Conferences, a college ministry aimed at 18-25 year olds. I was given one of their first worship CDs not long after their first album was recorded at their first conference in 1997, the year I got saved. You may be familiar with worship leaders like Chris Tomlin, David Crowder, Charlie Hall, or Kristian Stanfill who have all been raised up out of the Passion movement and ministry.

The founding and shaping verse of the Passion movement is found in **Isaiah 26:8**, particularly the last phrase:

> *Yes, Lord, walking in the way of your truth,*
>
> > *we wait for you;*
>
> > **your name and renown**
> >
> > **are the desire of our souls.**

Louie's focus and message on One Name—the name of Jesus—and the glory of God resonated deeply with me and fueled my faith in those early years and well past age 25. He also introduced me to the preaching and writing of John Piper—who's entire ministry has carefully thought, taught, and unpacked issues around "the glory of God."

The Westminster Shorter Catechism states, **"the chief end of man is to glorify God and enjoy Him forever."** Written in 1647, it has stood the test of time as a powerful articulation of the grand purpose and chief end of man's life according to the teaching of the Bible. Piper came along and, with theological precision, refined it even further by saying, "the purpose of man's life is to glorify God *by* enjoying Him forever."

One little tweak to one little word—massive implications.

Piper has given his life to unpacking the implications of that truth with a massive library of books, sermons, and written resources. He carefully shows how the two parts of the purpose of man are not actually two separate enterprises but one glorious life pursuit. To glorify God and to enjoy Him forever are inseparable and intrinsically linked.

If you really want to dig in deep and unpack these things, it will set you on a theological treadmill, pounding out biblical and theological miles, as you plumb the depths of the greatest theological minds in the history of the Church. It's a study and search that has deeply marked the leadership of Grace City Church and Stronger Man Nation and is built into the engine that still drives our same passion today. We say it now in our own way, but we cannot unsee it or unsay it.

## "GOD IS MOST GLORIFIED IN YOU WHEN YOU ARE MOST SATISFIED IN HIM" JOHN PIPER

The connection between God's glory and our pursuit of joy is forever fixed in Scripture. Piper coined the impactful sentence, "God is most glorified in you when you are most satisfied in Him." It's a mountain range and mouthful of glorious truth.

The whole pursuit of the Christian life becomes one of maximizing your joy in Christ as the primary way in which you glorify God. We do not glorify Him as mere self-denying, willpower-led, duty-driven servants. Instead, we most glorify Him as soul-satisfied, treasure-finding, heart-delighted, praise-erupting worshippers of God, who is the most glorious being in the universe!

Our joy in His glory is not optional. It is commanded. It matters very much where we find our joy. And it matters very much the way in which we glorify God. His glory, after all, is THE POINT.

We were made to get lost in wonder in the worship of God, to feel small yet loved in His presence. To enjoy making much of Him, not praising Him because we think He makes much of us. Sadly, there's a lot of that flying under the banner of cultural Christianity. Loving God because we think He is committed to making us great. God does not make much of us but rather frees us from needing to be made much of so that we can enjoy making much of Him forever. That's the proper orientation.

We were made to glorify Him by "seeing and savoring" the heart-satisfying beauty that is Jesus Christ. The understanding and experience of His grace causes the heart to spontaneously overflow with praise. This is good and right and freeing.

We experience this in the final seconds when our favorite team scores the game-winning touchdown. It would be impossible to fully glorify the reality of the moment and the victory of the team without freely expressing praise. The expression of praise completes the joy we long to express in that moment.

That's how it works with God. When our heart sees Him as the all-satisfying Savior He is, we praise Him! In that moment, all is right. God gets the glory and we get the joy—it's the best of all possible worlds. And this is how God has designed the Christian life to work.

His glory and our joy mingled in worship. Full-throttled praise and full-blown joy.

This is what it means to be ALL IN FOR ONE NAME. It's an urgent warning to repent of attempting to magnify our own name. It's a humbling tonic to the glory-seeking pride of men. It's a call to glorify Jesus with all our might. And it's an invitation to infinite joy. **ALL IN! ONE NAME!**

## Revevlation 4:9-11

*Whenever the living creatures give glory, honor and thanks to him who sits on the throne and who lives for ever and ever, the twenty-four elders fall down before him who sits on the throne and worship him who lives for ever and ever.*

*They lay their crowns before the throne and say:*

> *"You are worthy, our Lord and God,*
>
> *to receive glory and honor and power,*
>
> *for you created all things,*
>
> *and by your will they were created*
>
> *and have their being."*

"Talent is God given. Be humble.
Fame is man-given. Be grateful.
Conceit is self-given. Be careful."

— John Wooden

ATHLETE

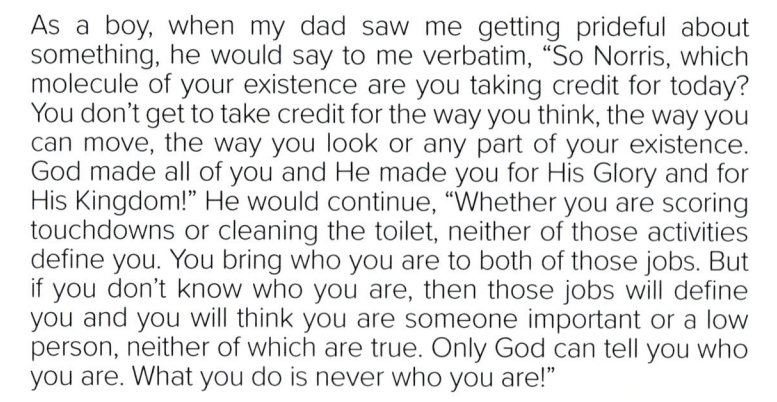

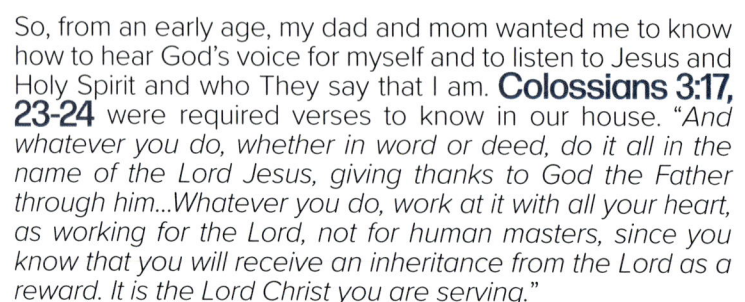

# FROM A STRONGER MAN

As a boy, when my dad saw me getting prideful about something, he would say to me verbatim, "So Norris, which molecule of your existence are you taking credit for today? You don't get to take credit for the way you think, the way you can move, the way you look or any part of your existence. God made all of you and He made you for His Glory and for His Kingdom!" He would continue, "Whether you are scoring touchdowns or cleaning the toilet, neither of those activities define you. You bring who you are to both of those jobs. But if you don't know who you are, then those jobs will define you and you will think you are someone important or a low person, neither of which are true. Only God can tell you who you are. What you do is never who you are!"

So, from an early age, my dad and mom wanted me to know how to hear God's voice for myself and to listen to Jesus and Holy Spirit and who They say that I am. **Colossians 3:17, 23-24** were required verses to know in our house. "*And whatever you do, whether in word or deed, do it all in the name of the Lord Jesus, giving thanks to God the Father through him...Whatever you do, work at it with all your heart, as working for the Lord, not for human masters, since you know that you will receive an inheritance from the Lord as a reward. It is the Lord Christ you are serving.*"

In all activities, including sports, God was the one who got the glory. God created me to love and experience physicality. The rougher things were the better I liked them. When I played football, I could somehow see the whole field in my head and make decisions on the fly. I experienced God's presence and pleasure while I was playing. Now, I am so old that Mike Holmgren was one of my high school football coaches. My senior year I was voted Most Valuable Football player in Northern CA. Coming out of high school I had scholarship offers to play football across the nation from Notre Dame to USC and many others. I chose Arizona State University not only to play but in order to meet my girlfriend Laurie Ann (God knew the real reason He sent me there). I was a 4-year starter at ASU. As a freshman, along with gymnast Scott Barclay (he is still the head gymnastics coach at ASU), we started the Fellowship of Christian Athletes program at ASU, and I led it as president for 4 years. It is still operating today. In one week in May, 1980, I graduated, married my Laurie Ann, and reported to rookie camp with the Pittsburg Steelers. We came home from rookie camp, finished our honeymoon (yahoo), and in the fall I reported back for training camp.

During the preseason of my rookie year, after making the team, I injured my back, and my legs went numb from the waist down. Doctors sat us down and said, "If your L5 vertebrae moves any more you are going to be paralyzed. You are all done playing football. No more riding horses, jumping up and down hard, or any activity that causes you to arch your back. Go get a desk job and be thankful you're still walking." So, from one moment to the next I could never again do so many of the things I loved to do. I shed some tears that day. I was sad to be injured, but my identity had already been made sure from God. I asked Him, "What's next? I know that my identity is not football player so where are You leading us now?" Laurie and I spent time on our knees making God's word a reality to be lived and not just verses to memorize. "Lord, we count it all joy in these hardships, we rejoice in all things, we give thanks in all things, we praise You in all things." The Trinity met us and spoke life into us even though the pain did not go away.

**What an amazing adventure life continues to be. I praise God for parents that settled the glory issue for me when I was a boy. I have been all in for one name since 1970.** Whatever God has made you good at, whatever it is that you love to do, whatever way your brain works and processes information, whatever way you bring creativity and beauty to the world, whatever gift you bring to the world in your uniqueness, whatever pain, suffering, and hardship you have and will endure—cast these crowns before the throne and with the 24 elders fall down and worship and say, "*You are worthy, our Lord and God!*"

> *Each of the four living creatures had six wings and was covered with eyes all around, even under its wings. Day and night they never stop saying:*
>
> *'Holy, holy, holy is the Lord God Almighty, who was, and is, and is to come.'*
>
> *Whenever the living creatures give glory, honor and thanks to him who sits on the throne and who lives for ever and ever, the twenty-four elders fall down before him who sits on the throne and worship him who lives for ever and ever. They lay their crowns before the throne and say:*
>
> *'You are worthy, our Lord and God,*
> *to receive glory and honor and power,*
> *for you created all things,*
> *and by your will they were created*
> *and have their being.'*
> **Revelation 4:8-11**

# Norris, 65

# REFLECT & DISCUSS

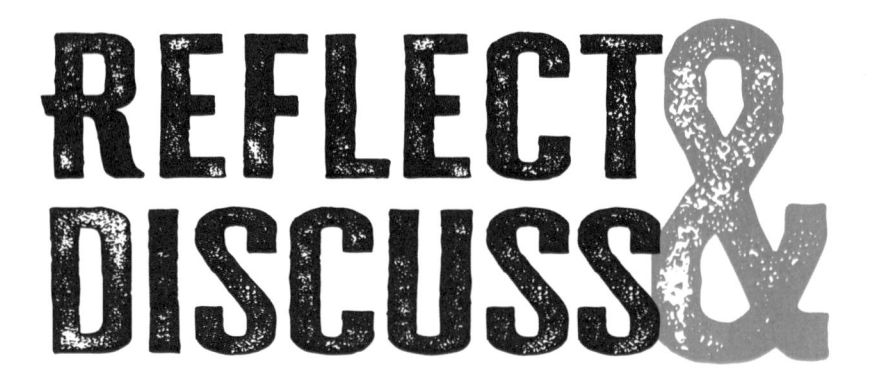

1. What is your biggest takeaway from this chapter? From the testimony?

2. What's the most significant award or recognition you've been given? What was that like?

3. Why is it so crucial to settle the glory issue in our minds and hearts? How can you "settle the glory issue?" What does that involve?

4. We were made to worship. It's not a matter of *if* but *who* or *what*. Like a garden hose stuck on or a billboard on display, our hearts are always worshipping something or someone. Is this a new understanding of "worship" for you? Why is this a helpful way to look at it? What are the implications for our lives?

5. How has God lovingly "put you in your place" and reminded you "it's not about you?" Do you have any examples from your life experience of how you've learned or been taught that it's not about you? What happens when we try to make it about us?

_____
_____
_____

6. *"God is most glorified in you when you are most satisfied in Him."* What is helpful about this quote? What questions and/or thoughts does it bring up?

_____
_____
_____

7. How would you describe what it means to live "All In for One Name" in your own words? What are some Biblical passages that reinforce this mindset? (Here are a few to check out: 1 Cor. 10:31; 1 Peter 4:11; Isa. 42:8; Isa. 43:7; Eph. 1:3-14; Jude 1:24; Rev. 4:1-11; Rev. 5:11-14; Rev. 7:9-12)

_____
_____
_____

# TAKE ACTION

- Write out a personal prayer and declaration for your life that encapsulates your desire to be a stronger man—a leader who lives "All In for One Name." How do you want to lead and impact others? How do you want to serve the Lord and be used by Him? Include what you are most grateful for to the Lord and ask for His grace and strength to help you run the race, finish strong, receive the crown, and bring glory to Him in all you do.

- What is the single greatest insight, encouragement, reminder, or takeaway you have received from this 12-week study? What was most helpful in general? Who could you share this with in your life?

# ADDITIONAL QUESTIONS FOR DISCUSSION

1. What's the best sports experience you've ever had? What's the worst?

2. If you could meet any famous athlete from any period of time who would it be and why?

3. Who is the best leader you've known in your life? Why? What was it about them that made them a great leader?

4. Who were some of your favorite sports teams and players growing up? Who are your favorites today?

5. What are the benefits of youth sports experiences? What are the dangers/pitfalls?

6. How would you describe the positives and negatives of professional sports today?

7. In what ways would you want to emulate attributes and qualities of manhood from your father?

8. In what ways would you NOT want to emulate attributes and qualities of manhood from your father?

9. How would you describe the kind of legacy you want to leave? What words do you hope others use to describe your impact?

10. Share a version of your spiritual history and journey.

11. What were your first experiences of church like?

12. What would you say is the biggest current hurdle or obstacle in your life?

13. What weighs on your mind/heart the most these days?

14. What changes are needed in your current family routine (daily, weekly, monthly)?

15. What do you do for fun? What do you do with your family for fun?

16. Are you satisfied with your current level of availability and connection with your wife and kids? What would improve it?

17. Are you satisfied with your current relationship with God? What would improve it?

18. If you could meet and spend an hour with anyone in history—who would it be and why? Who would be in your Top 5.

19. What current living leader would you most want to spend a day shadowing and why?

20. If you could talk to your 18-year-old self, what would you say? What counsel/advice would you give yourself? (To a young man reading this: What advice would you give yourself 2 years ago?)

# WAYS TO PRACTICE BEING AN ATHLETE / LEADER

- Clearly articulate a life vision, mission, purpose statement. Know where you're going and go there.

- Clearly articulate core values for yourself and your family. Involve them in the process. Know the kind of person and family you want to be and pursue it.

- Finish what you start.

- Initiate the process of helping each person in your family make a personal plan for growth in each area of life. Lead by example.

- Pursue a sustainable lifestyle of physical fitness and strength.

- Take responsibility to do the bulk of the driving with your wife and family.

- Lead your family to connect with a local church.

- Initiate leading prayer in your home.

- Pray with and for your wife out loud, every day.

- Pray with each of your children out loud, every day.

- Lead the sharing of "highs and lows" with your family to reflect on each day, month, quarter, and year.

- Facilitate constructive conversation and evaluation of how things are going as a family. What's going well? Where do we need to improve?

- Build a healthy sense of "team" with your family, employees, at your place of work.

- Prioritize using fun experiences or projects to forge bonds of deep relational history and fun memories.

- Plan and lead fun trips and vacations with and for your family.

- Gather a group of dads and sons to do fun outings and activities together.

- Do your best at whatever you do.

- Do hard things.

- Read, read, read. Readers are leaders and leaders are readers. Cultivate a love for reading in your home.

- Read good biographies of great historical leaders and events. Share and discuss them with your family.

- Watch the iconic sports movies that exemplify great character qualities and life lessons. Facilitate discussion and dialogue about each movie.

"Have nothing to do with godless myths and old wives' tales; rather, train yourself to be godly. For physical training is of some value, but godliness has value for all things, holding promise for both the present life and the life to come."

— I Timothy 4:7-8